MW01033204

MADE
IN
OCCUPIED
JAPAN:
A Collector's Guide

Also by Marian Klamkin

Flower Arrangements That Last
Flower Arranging for Period Decoration
The Collector's Book of Boxes
The Collector's Book of Art Nouveau
The Collector's Book of Wedgwood
The Collector's Book of Bottles
Hands to Work: Shaker Folk Art and Industries
White House China
American Patriotic and Political China
The Return of Lafayette 1824–1825
Picture Postcards
The Collector's Guide to Depression Glass
The Depression Glass Collector's Price Guide
Old Sheet Music: A Pictorial History
Marine Antiques
The Collector's Guide to Carnival Glass

With Charles Klamkin

Wood Carvings: North American Folk Sculptures
Investing in Antiques and Popular Collectibles for Pleasure and Profit

MADE IN OCCUPIED JAPAN:

A Collector's Guide

Marian Klamkin

Photographs by Charles Klamkin

CROWN PUBLISHERS, INC.   NEW YORK

Copyright © 1976 by Marian Klamkin

All rights reserved. No part of this book may be reproduced or utilized in any form or by any means, electronic or mechanical, including photocopying, recording, or by any informa- tion storage and retrieval system, without permission in writing from the Publisher. Inquiries should be addressed to Crown Publishers, Inc., One Park Avenue, New York, N.Y. 10016.

Printed in the United States of America

Published simultaneously in Canada by General Publishing Company Limited

Library of Congress Cataloging in Publication Data

Klamkin, Marian.
    Made in Occupied Japan.

    Includes index.
    1. Japan—History—Allied occupation, 1945–1952—Collectibles. 2. Art industries and trade—Japan.
I. Title.
NK1071.K6   1976   680   76-17007
ISBN 0-517-52660-3
ISBN 0-517-52661-1 pbk.

Designed by Deborah Daly

Acknowledgments

Without the help, enthusiasm, and hospitality of Joseph P. Valenti and his wife, Rachel, this book would not have been written. Access to the Valenti collection of objects made in Occupied Japan was necessary to the research, writing, and photography for this book, and the Valentis made all of the work an enjoyable experience. Unless otherwise identified, all the objects pictured in this book are from the Valenti collection.

I am grateful, also, to many others whose objects appear on the following pages. Many collectors and dealers were generous and helpful in making their possessions available for photographing.

Photographs of pages from a 1950 catalog of the General Merchandising Company of New York appear in various chapters of the book. For permission to photograph the only available catalog I thank Mr. Milton Shaw, president of the company.

Contents

1

Introduction to Collectibles Made in Occupied Japan

Collecting has become a popular pastime in the United States. The collector selects a category of antique articles, or of objects that are less than antique, that appeals to him, and then spends his leisure hours and surplus funds in seeking items that fit into this special field of interest. Many Americans specialize in a collecting category related to their country's history. One of the newest, fastest-growing, and most popular of such categories consists of those objects made in Japan for export to the United States during the period of the American Occupation following World War II.

For a collectible to become widely popular it must have certain characteristics. First, it must be available nationwide in some quantity so that it is not next to impossible to find; yet it should not be so plentiful that the search is boringly easy. There should be some variety within the collecting category too, so that all collections will not be exactly like one another. If the objects collected are representative of an important period in American or world history, they will have special appeal to many people. Another desirable criterion might be that objects are available at varied prices; often a beginning collector cannot afford to risk the larger sums that a more experienced collector knows would be well invested—after all, all collectors like to feel that what they own will appreciate in value within a reasonable amount of time. Finally, it is especially helpful if the objects collected are not too space-consuming and are attractive when displayed in the home.

Merchandise made for export during the American Occupation of Japan seems to satisfy all the above criteria for thousands of American collectors. To them, the initials "O.J." do not denote a popular citrus fruit drink or a running back for the Buffalo Bills. "O.J.," in the world of popular collectibles, is the abbreviation for all products marked "Made in Occupied Japan" or simply "Occupied Japan." This mark identifies all objects made for export to the United States during a rather short period of about five years. Although the Occupation lasted for six and a half years, trade did not begin immediately after the war ended, and as soon as the peace treaty with Japan was signed the mark became obsolete.

An extremely wide variety of collectibles was marked "Made in Occupied Japan." Many things were made for only a short period of time and in limited amounts, but others were produced by the hundreds of thousands. In their effort to rebuild international trade following the war the Japanese produced a broad range of products, most of which were shipped to the United States. Although most collectors believe that the "Occupied Japan" collectibles they own were made during the entire period of the Occupation, from September 2, 1945, to April 28, 1952, evidence will be offered in the following chapter that proves them wrong. Actually, these marked pieces of porcelain, pottery, paper, metal, cloth, glass, celluloid, wood, and plastic represent at best only five years of Japanese production. Some of them were of exceptionally good quality; many others were dime-store items that sold for pennies.

Although the largest proportion of "Made in Occupied Japan" merchandise was comprised of porcelain figurines, pottery kitchen novelties, and dishes, the Japanese made hundreds of other consumer products to sell to the American market. Today, a determined collector can still find toys, dolls, baby clothes, artists' paintbrushes, pencils, erasers, Christmas tree ornaments and lights, novelty cigarette lighters, metal ashtrays, paper and cloth fans, parasols, glassware, vacuum bottles, clocks, watches, cameras, binoculars, pincushions and other sewing paraphernalia, lamps, rulers, and countless other items—the list is almost endless.

There was some resistance to these Japanese-made products when they first began to arrive on American shores. Many American manufacturers who were retooling for peacetime production resented competition from a former enemy, and so certain products were made for an even shorter period of time than five years. The punitive "Made in Occupied Japan" mark made the Japanese goods easy to identify, and the mark was carefully policed by American customs officials both at the ports of entry and as far down as the store level. In American wholesalers' catalogs all Japanese products were carefully identified. Nevertheless, there were American customers for most of the Japanese products made for export. The prices of both decorative and useful merchandise were so much lower than for comparable products made elsewhere that even superpatriots found the Japanese goods hard to resist. The Japanese were also astute enough to make many of their porcelain figurines in shapes that would appeal to Americans, such as their "Uncle Sam" or cowboy or cowgirl figures.

Many "Made in Occupied Japan" collectibles can still be found in flea markets throughout the United States. They are, after all, only a little more than a quarter of a century old. The better-quality bisque and porcelain items and the scarce lacquer pieces can now be purchased in antique shops even though they are far from being truly "antique." The collectibles still to be found at fairly reasonable prices in flea markets, garage sales, and tag sales are mostly the smaller, inferior porcelain figures, salt and pepper shakers, or miniature vases that once were sold wholesale for sixty-five cents a dozen. These tiny novelties were made in huge quantity, but many were broken or thrown out, and so even sophisticated collectors are buying all they can find that are still in good condition. Percentagewise, no other category of collectible has risen so rapidly in value in so short a time.

Objects made for export during the Occupation of Japan vary enormously today not only in quantity but also in market price. Many of the bisque figurines were carefully molded and hand decorated. When these better examples are found in mint condition, they become the most valued items in an "Occupied Japan" collection. The larger, well-detailed glazed porcelain figurines, also very desirable, are destined to keep appreciating in value as the number of collectors increases and the supply dwindles. Most of the better figurines were made and sold in pairs, and collectors often find it difficult to obtain complete sets. Good-quality dinner sets, tea services, and dessert sets are also difficult to obtain with all pieces intact.

Lacquerware, made in limited quantity during the Occupation, is another premium collectible. Americans did not understand the process of lacquer production, and many potential customers would not believe that objects made on a wood core could be impervious to liquor or other beverages. However, a few importers who were impressed by the amount of hand labor and artistry that went into good-quality lacquerware invested in it heavily even though, in spite of the low postwar Japanese wages, lacquer was expensive by the time it reached the gift shops; there was also the strong customer resistance to it. Not a great deal of lacquer was made in comparison to the amount of pottery and porcelain, and since it is in short supply it is finally bringing prices among today's collectors that it could never command when it was new.

Some of the novelty items made for export to the United States during the Occupation are very revealing of the Japanese notion of the American mentality. Among the peculiar porcelain and bisque objects made were many that showed what can only be described as a rather low-class bathroom humor. Miniature toilets, tiny outhouses, and porcelain potties are common examples. Figurines of all the world's national groups and races were made too, but unfortunately most of the black figures are caricatures that indicate the Japanese were aware of the American prejudices that prevailed only a quarter century ago. Cheap souvenir items were made by the thousands to satisfy the American tourists' habit of buying mementos to remind themselves and their neighbors of where they had been.

Although thousands of new products were designed in Japan for export to the

United States during the Occupation, many of the postwar products had been made before 1940 and had proved successful then. No other country could produce the wonderful paper novelties that American children had played with and loved in the period before the war. For example, intricately accordion-folded and pasted tissue-paper fans and ornaments were again available after the war. Prewar children remembered the polished clamshells that, when immersed in a glass of water, would open up to display a magic garden of paper flowers, green foliage, and a tiny American flag. These were once again available for a new generation of American children. Similar shells, now made in Korea, are poor imitations of the original Japanese product. Miniature paper parasols are still available, but most of them are now made in Korea or Taiwan and do not compare with the Japanese product. Because paper collectibles are ephemeral, they are high on any collector's list of desirable objects; when marked "Made in Occupied Japan," they can bring prices many times the original cost.

It is undeniable that many "Made in Occupied Japan" collectibles are of obviously poor workmanship, but hundreds of others were artistically designed and carefully made. Frequently collectors specialize in just one or two categories of "Occupied Japan" objects. Some collectors search for only the imaginative, well-made ones. One collector may choose to concentrate on mechanical toys; another may buy only celluloid dolls and other toys. There are specialists who accumulate all the miniature tea sets and doll dishes they can find, and still others who search for cups and saucers of paper-thin porcelain that were produced in a huge variety of shapes, sizes, ond styles of decoration. Many collectors look for the tiny bisque shelf-sitter figures, whereas others want only the optical equipment made by the Japanese.

The collector who decides to specialize in glass objects made for export by the Japanese will find that his collection grows very slowly. Very little glass was made simply because Japanese glassmakers could not compete with American and European manufacturers of similar products. The United States has always been a glass-producing nation; it is also likely that manufacturers on this side of the Pacific Ocean were not happy to have competition from their former enemies. Therefore, glass embossed with the "Made in Occupied Japan" mark is a rarity. Cologne bottles in the Art Deco style of the 1930s seem to be the most easily found of the glass objects.

The Japanese, not unaware of the probable strong American resistance to their products, attempted to make much of their pottery and porcelain closely resembling the products of European manufacturers. Blue and white jasperware ashtrays and cigarette boxes—a novice collector may mistake these for Wedgwood—may be a "Made in Occupied Japan" imitation. A brown-glazed "Rockingham" teapot that looks like a twin to the traditional English product may easily have the telltale mark. A figurine that at first glance looks like a Hummel product may well be Japan's less expensive imitation. If the Japanese developed a reputation for being great "borrowers" of art styles during the Occupation, it is because they understood the necessity for making products that did not look "Japanese." The type of porcelain most difficult for O.J. collectors to find is that which is decorated in the traditional Japanese style with which Americans were familiar long before hostilities commenced between the two countries. Although many of the porcelain figurines appear in Oriental costume, few of these are in Japanese attire—most of the clothing is Chinese, Korean, or Siamese.

Very little of the porcelain or bisque made for export during the Occupation is of a quality that can be considered fine art. The best and most expensive of the figurines do not compare in detail, decoration, or quality with their German, French, Austrian, or English prototypes. However, they did not cost as much either, when they were new, and most have a certain popular appeal and charm that once made them welcome inexpensive decorations in American homes.

Collecting objects marked "Made in Occupied Japan" promises to continue to grow in popular appeal in the future. Many of the smaller collectibles that were once plentiful at flea markets across the nation are becoming scarce, as astute collectors and dealers buy everything they can still find at reasonable prices. Some of the more desirable collectibles have already been priced at hundreds of times their original cost. For instance, a 3½-inch bisque doll that wholesaled for three dollars a gross now costs several times that amount for just one doll.

There is such a wide variety of objects marked "Made in Occupied Japan" that no single collector could manage to gather a sample of everything that was made. Thousands of objects have already been identified and illustrated in the several price guides that have been published, and many others are illustrated on the following pages. However, there are still many undiscovered surprises in store for the diligent and persistent collector. Never fail to turn over all pottery, glass, wood, metal, and paper objects that might be marked "Occupied Japan." It is also necessary to become familiar with the various products marked with a paper sticker, which may have been removed or fallen off. Many such objects that look as though they belong in your collection will be marked only "Made in Japan" or "Japan." These may have been made during the Occupation, but without proof they should be rejected.

When any collectible category becomes popular and the demand becomes high enough, collectors always become concerned that the objects they seek may have been duplicated and bear a counterfeit mark. This is a special concern of "Occupied Japan" collectors, since they are really collecting a mark rather than the objects. Because of this, collectors have been warned not to purchase anything before they have "tested" the mark by wetting a finger and trying to rub it out. One writer has even gone so far as to suggest that any suspicious mark on pottery or porcelain be tested with a lacquer solvent such as nail-polish remover. If these suggestions are followed, some good authentic collectibles will be relegated to the back shelves of dealers' shops. There is evidence that many "Made in Occupied Japan" marks were stamped on products that slipped through customs and were marked at the store level. This seldom happened with the better-quality products; the easily removable stamped mark is most often found on tiny bisque items that had little value when new. Most marks, however, are genuine and will not come off.

Obviously, the search is on for all objects made in Occupied Japan for export to the United States. Some can be found in unlikely places. A rubber eraser or pencil stuck in the back of a desk drawer may be marked "Made in Occupied Japan." The packet of needles in Grandmother's sewing box may be a desirable collectible, and the tomato-shaped pincushion or the velvet strawberry emery may have a tiny cloth label that reads "Occupied Japan." The sewing box itself may be worth checking as well. If you inspect the backs of all the miniature bisque and celluloid dolls you can find at antique shows and flea markets, perhaps one out of a hundred will have "Made in Occupied Japan" embossed on it.

The old fishbowl ornaments that are packed away in the back of a closet may turn out to be most desirable collectibles if they were bought at the right time. The fan you won at an amusement park in the late forties or early fifties may be more valuable than you thought. The possibilities for discovering "Made in Occupied Japan" collectibles are almost limitless. If your father happened to have saved a squirting lapel flower or a cigar that explodes to reveal the Stars and Stripes, from some postwar convention, it is likely that these too may be marked "Occupied Japan." No one can say the Japanese did not understand their customers.

2

History of Objects Made in Occupied Japan

Although the Occupation of Japan began officially on September 2, 1945, shortly after the meeting on the battleship *Missouri* in Tokyo Bay, where the terms of surrender were signed, it was a long time following that historic event before goods for export were shipped out. Japan remained a closed country for almost two years while General Douglas MacArthur directed the immediate tasks of feeding and housing the Japanese. The rebuilding of industries was a priority also, but there were many hurdles to be overcome before it could take place.

The earliest attitude of the American government and of many of its people was a hostile one that was to be expected in a post-surrender period. There was talk of reparations, and many Americans favored keeping the Japanese to a cost of living that would be a minimal level of subsistence. In the early days of the Occupation, the pattern of recovery was limited by the wording in the Potsdam Agreement: "Japan shall be permitted to maintain such industries as will sustain her economy and permit of just reparations in kind, but not those which would enable her to rearm for war."

Industrial managers were reluctant to reopen factories that had been closed since the end of the war. No one had defined for them exactly what reparations would be necessary, and it was assumed that expensive machines would be confiscated. Goods were imported only to the level that they would prevent famine and disease or secure raw materials necessary to manufacture products needed by the Occupation forces. Some goods were imported that would be necessary to the manufacture of products that would eventually be exported to help establish a balance of trade.

Lee R. Fleming, chief of the export-import division of SCAP's (Supreme Commander, Allied Powers) Economic and Scientific Section, announced in 1946 that "available exports are programmed in ratio to Japan's prewar trading pattern." There were exceptions to this program, however. One was that exports that were in world short supply were allocated by a combined committee in Washington to countries that stated requirements and were able to purchase their allotments on terms agreeable to the supplying nations. The second was exports that were bartered for essential imports.

In 1946, Japan was averaging a foreign trade balance of $24,000,000 every six months shortly after business with other countries resumed. Exports at that time consisted mainly of coal, mining supplies, raw silk, mulberry seedlings, silkworm eggs, and various light manufactures. These were sold to purchase food, medical supplies, phosphate rock, petroleum products, and salt. Later, the Japanese were to send hundreds of thousands of salt and pepper shakers to their chief customer, the United States.

One of General MacArthur's tasks was to increase the flow of goods into and out of Japan; all trade was controlled by his office. On March 4, 1947, the *New York Times* reported that the American government had abolished Treasury licenses under the Trading with the Enemy Act and that authority rested with the theater commanders. "Restrictions remain intact," the *Times* reported; "the action made little difference in procedure." American and British traders had been free since January 1, 1947, to communicate with prewar suppliers in Japan but could not enter into contracts or discuss prices.

American businessmen and traders from other nations had been poised in Shanghai for months waiting for restrictions to be lifted so that they could move into Japan, but MacArthur insisted that there was no room in his plans for "foreign exploitation." He demanded—and had—complete control. Meanwhile, many American Occupation soldiers were being approached by Japan's industrialists and urged to take part in some facet of trade between Japan and the United States, once it was opened. Many men in uniform made arrangements with heads of Japanese manufacturing firms that led to lucrative jobs in the export trade once the American soldier was back in the States. For some GI's the Japanese contacts proved invaluable. Many others invested time and money in business deals that were disastrous.

On June 10, 1947, MacArthur announced that Japan was ready to resume foreign trade and that, on August 15, 1947, private buyers would be permitted to enter Japan. Business transactions would be allowed after September 1. MacArthur realized the necessity of removing economic blockades, and he said, "Japan's economy will remain precarious until trade is restored to normal channels, which means private trade channels." At the time, he said he realized the measure was merely palliative but it was the best that could be done until peace was declared.

To today's collectors of objects marked "Made in Occupied Japan," perhaps the most significant headline concerning the importation of Japanese goods appeared in the business section of the *New York Times* on August 10, 1948. It read: JAPANESE WARES HERE IN QUANTITY. *Now Labeled Made in Occupied Japan—Resistance Met But Not Because of Prices.*

The article said that Japanese products "of the kind widely boycotted before the war" were beginning to make their first appearance in local variety stores. Sales clerks reported that the goods were meeting some buyer resistance, but not because of the prices. Although the prices for Japanese goods had been notoriously low in the pre-Pearl Harbor era, they reflected the well-known effects of inflation. The *Times* went on: "Articles such as fans, trinket boxes, tiny vases and toy china sets are selling for three and four times the pre-war rates. All are marked 'Made in Occupied Japan.' "

The newspaper reporter had interviewed a clerk in one of the F. W. Woolworth's Fifth Avenue stores, where the goods were being sold in the basement. The clerk explained that customer reaction took three forms. Some, she said, appeared to be unaware that the articles were Japanese, and some were indifferent when they recognized their origin. Others, proclaiming themselves veterans or relatives of dead servicemen or former prisoners of war, showed open antagonism.

The *Times* reporter had also interviewed an official of the Supreme Commander, Allied Powers, Foreign Trade office in New York, who said that the Occupation administration was encouraging the export of these and other products to this country from Japan as a means of speeding the conquered country's recovery. The SCAP office in New York was the representative of the United States Army for coordinating private trade with Japan.

The SCAP official blamed the increased prices on high wages and inflation, but the objects listed were mostly inexpensive items to begin with. It would seem that better-quality Japanese goods were later imports.

For most of the "Occupied Japan" objects being collected today, the earliest date of arrival in American stores appears to have been August, 1948. The *Times* article is important, since it seems to be the earliest evidence that everything *was* marked "Made in Occupied Japan." The mark did not make it easier for American stores to sell the products.

Consumer products from Japan continued to meet with some resistance on the American market. On January 4, 1950, the *Times* announced that the Japanese government was completing plans for the establishment in the United States of its first semidiplomatic representation since the war by opening offices in New York, Chicago, and San Francisco to increase Japanese trade. By this time Japan's industrial production had reached 79.5 percent of the 1932–36 level, the last five-year period before the outbreak of the Sino-Japanese War. This figure reached 95 percent with the inclusion of utilities production. It was pointed out by the *Times* that this was achieved with a United States subsidy of more than a billion dollars since the surrender.

By July 16, 1950, the Japanese Overseas Agency was open for business with an office at 60 East Forty-second Street in New York and other offices in San Francisco, Los Angeles, Seattle, and Honolulu. "In some respects," said the *Times,* "the operation resembles an unofficial consulate service." Its primary purpose was to develop more private business in exporting and importing, an important requirement in stabilizing Japan's economy.

One of the biggest problems Japan had hoped to overcome by establishing American offices for trade was that of changing the American's conception of Japanese goods as "cheap," by the promotion of higher-priced merchandise. Mr. Kohei Teraoka, director of the New York office, said, "Although announcement of the agency has brought in a good quantity of buying inquiries, outbreak of the Korean conflict, with its implications of more economic aid to Japan, is causing Japanese merchants to hold back in expectation of higher prices on the American market. A report that this is most unlikely is being sent to Tokyo." Mr. Teraoka also reported that Americans had complaints against Japanese exporters, but he did not elaborate on this statement. Importers in the United States were evidently concerned that the Japanese would not be able to match the quality of the sample products shown them. As collectors of Occupied Japanese goods are aware today, many products of very good quality were made. It is evident from the above that most of these were items made from 1950 to the end of the Occupation.

If the United States was to accept Japanese consumer goods, the wholesalers and the press had to be made aware of what was to become available. On April 11, 1950, the *New York Times* reported: 1,000 ITEMS OF TRADE IN JAPANESE DISPLAY. This was the second such trade show that was held. The first, held in August of 1949, included such items as garden tools, musical instruments, sewing machines, clothing, and knit gloves. The merchandise was owned by Northwest Airlines, which sponsored the trade show.

The exhibit on April 11 was assembled by the Osaka Foreign Trade Institute in New York, at SCAP headquarters foreign trade office at 11 West Forty-second Street. It consisted mainly of variety store items, Christmas novelties, buttons, beads, hammered metalware, small brass animals, and fishing equipment. Some children's boudoir sets were shown also.

The above items, then, were the first documented consumer goods to reach these shores from Japan following the war. Thus, for only three or four years, the better consumer items were on the American market with the "Made in Occupied Japan" mark. In the twenty-five years since that time, many of the items have been worn out, broken, or thrown away. This is why, only a few years ago, there seemed to be enough items still to be found to satisfy the early collectors of "Occupied Japan" items. However, once collectors began to buy everything they could find, fewer and fewer items remained on the market—and today the collector really has to search for the prime items, such as the better-quality bisque or porcelain figures or good-quality tea sets. For many years to come, though, there will be constant surprises—novelty items that are marked "Made in Occupied Japan" and that have not been noted previous-ly—as collectors also search for the undocumented and unusual objects; all of them represent an interesting phase of American and Japanese history.

3

Marks

The story of the marks on objects made in Occupied Japan is a confusing one. There are perhaps at least over one hundred marks to be found on porcelain and pottery, and many of these are marks of companies no longer in existence or marks of the importer rather than the manufacturer. Certain marks have become associated with high-grade china. For instance, the mark "Andrea" is sometimes found on figurines in bisque that are well modeled and of good quality. By far the most prevalent mark is simply the stamped legend "Made in Occupied Japan."

Those Japanese who had made products for export to the United States before World War II had become accustomed to marking their wares according to United States law. The McKinley Tariff Act, passed in October, 1890, stipulated that all objects imported from abroad had to be marked with the name of the country of origin printed in English. The Japanese identified most of their wares with the word "Nippon," the English version of their word for their own country. This seems to have been unsatisfactory to the American lawmakers, and in 1921 the United States Treasury decreed that the Japanese were not adhering to the law and that they must use the word "Japan" rather than "Nippon." Therefore, collectors of prewar Japanese pottery and porcelain have little trouble dating their pieces.

Confusion in marks does exist for Japanese products imported once trade was resumed following World War II. The United States Bureau of Customs ruling T.D. 52162(2) reads:

> "Made in Occupied Japan," "Made in Japan," "Japan," or "Occupied Japan" are acceptable markings to indicate the name of the country of origin under the marking provision of the Tariff Act of 1930, as amended, of articles manufactured or produced in Japan.
> *Bureau letter to collector of Customs, Los Angeles, California, February 18, 1949*

It would seem from the above that the "Made in Occupied Japan" or "Occupied Japan" was optional, but this does not appear to have been the case. Objects can be found that were probably goods left from before the war and that had already been marked "Japan" to which the words "Made in Occupied Japan" were added. Certainly, many exporters used the full mark to be on the safe side, and often the mark appears on an object more than once. It is probable that U.S. Customs officials were somewhat punitive, and in order to prevent shipments of goods from being sent back for further marking the Japanese used the full four-word legend most often. Methods of marking varied with the type of material used, and many wood, glass, and paper products were marked with a printed paper sticker.

1–60. Marks found on bisque, porcelain, and pottery objects. Undoubtedly there are many others.

CMC
MADE IN OCCUPIED
JAPAN

CHUGAI CHINA
MADE IN
OCCUPIED JAPAN

CHUGAI CHINA
MADE IN
OCCUPIED JAPAN

MADE N OCCUPIED
JAPAN

MADE IN
OCCUPIED
JAPAN

MADE IN
OCCUPIED
JAPAN

HAND PAINTED
CHASE
MADE IN
OCCUPIED JAPAN

CHUBU CHINA
OCCUPIED
JAPAN

MADE IN
CROCKERY
IMPORTERS
OCCUPIED JAPAN

MADE IN OCCUPIED
JAPAN

E.W
MADE IN
OCCUPIED
JAPAN

MADE IN
OCCUPIED JAPAN

HAND PAIIITED
MADE IN
OCCUPIED
JAPAN

Hand Painted
MADE IND
OCCUPIED
JAPAN

FAIRYLAND CHINA
HAND PAINTED
MADE IN OCCUPIED
JAPAN

G E C
MADE IN OCCUPIED
JAPAN

GOLD CASTLE
MADE IN
OCCUPIED JAPAN
REG

HAND PAINTED
MADE IN
OCCUPIED
JAPAN

H. KATO
MADE IN
OCCUPIED
JAPAN

H KATO
MADE IN
OCCUPIED
JAPAN

H
Hokutosha
MADE IN
OCCUPIED JAPAN

Hand Painted
K
MADE IN
OCCUPIED JAPAN

D
OCCUPIED

K. ISHIHARA
MADE IN
OCCUPIED
JAPAN

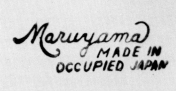

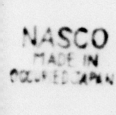

NASCO
MADE IN
OCCUPIED JAPAN

OCCUPIED
JAPAN

OHASHI CHINA
K
MADE IN
OCCUPIED JAPAN

ORION
MADE IN JAPAN
OCCUPIED

Hand Painted
ORION
CHINA
MADE IN
OCCUPIED JAPAN

PAULUX
MADE IN
OCCUPIED JAPAN

ROYAL SEALY
MADE IN OCCUPIED JAPAN

S.G.K.
CHINA
MADE IN OCCUPIED
JAPAN

SONE
CHINA
MADE IN
OCCUPIED
JAPAN

HAND PAINTED
TRIMONT
CHINA
MADE IN
OCCUPIED JAPAN

OCCUPIED
T
JAPAN

TORII BRAND
MADE IN OCCUPIED
JAPAN

When the *New York Times* reported, on August 10, 1948, that Japanese wares had arrived in New York in quantity, they also noted: "All are marked 'Made in Occupied Japan.'" Further indications that more goods were marked that way than not is the recollection of a store manager for the Kresge chain, who was in charge of checking every piece of Japanese merchandise coming into his store. He was given a rubber stamp with the words "Made in Occupied Japan" so that he could stamp any pieces that had not been previously marked. It is evident from this story that some pieces now believed to be "fake" by many collectors are not that. They just received their stamping in stores in this country. By attempting to remove marks that are stamped over the glaze on some porcelain pieces, the overwary collector is ruining some otherwise identifiable pieces of postwar Japanese products.

The "Made in Occupied Japan" and "Occupied Japan" marks are the only ones that have significance for collectors of Japanese postwar objects. The mark may be printed, impressed, embossed, stamped, acid etched, or—in a few cases—handwritten. Often the mark may have been placed only on the box in which an object was packed. Additional marks will be customs inspectors' stamps and various other export or import regulatory marks. Usually, as in the case of a package of identical pieces of china, the box and every piece inside will have the "Occupied" mark. Once in a while, one or two small items of a group that was packed together will not be marked. For instance, miniature teacups may have been too small to stamp and only the larger pieces of a set such as the teapot will have the mark.

Most of the high-grade porcelain and bisque were late imports, and some of these are found with the mark seemingly scraped off. Collectors have assumed that this was done after the products were in the United States, so that dealers could pass off the figurines as German or French imports and therefore sell them at a higher price. This is unlikely. Most of the pieces of this type have an oblong unglazed panel on their base, and the mark, usually acid etched in script, can be clearly seen if the piece is held at an angle to the light. This type of marking was probably used toward the end of the Occupation, and possibly by this time Customs had become more tolerant. Also, because the mark is not easy to see, American merchants could buy goods near the end of the Occupation on which the telltale mark was not too obvious.

62. Mark from a small bisque figurine. Usually the smaller items are marked only "Occupied Japan" or "Made in Occupied Japan."

61. Mark and original retail price for pottery wall plaque of Dutch figure.

63. Raised mark is unusual; this one can be seen only on glazed pottery pieces.

64. Raised mark on the bottom of a cologne bottle.

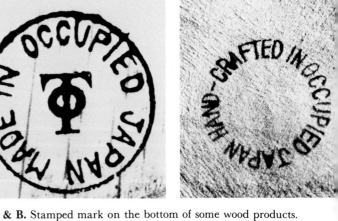

65. Circular mark on the bottom of a pressed glass mustard jar.

66 A & B. Stamped mark on the bottom of some wood products.

If the "Occupied" marks are confusing, the manufacturers' marks on cups, saucers, teapots, and other chinaware are even more so for the novice collector. Some of the marks were meant to confuse the customer. The Japanese were well aware of the resistance of many Americans to their products, and their chinaware marks, especially, seem to have been designed with the myopic reader in mind. "Sone" and "Tone" china were brands that looked like "Bone" china at a glance. "Royal Sealy" is not a name one might associate with Japan, and "Fairyland" china is the name of a type of iridescent bone china made by Wedgwood in the 1920s and 1930s. "Paulux" and "Chase" are not names that sound Japanese either. In these trademarks, the "Made in Occupied Japan" or "Occupied Japan" is usually printed in very small letters.

67. Mark found on metal objects.

68. Mark found on metal objects.

The truth is that only a few brand names used by the manufacturers of dishes have much meaning for the collector. The most outstanding name is, of course, "Noritake." This is found only on better-quality dishes, but it is probable that the same company made many of the other "Occupied" tea sets, dinnerware, and demitasse sets that were shipped under other brand names. Many pieces of chinaware of very good quality can be found that have no manufacturers' mark at all. This does not detract from the value of the pieces as long as the "Occupied" mark is there.

Most "Made in Occupied Japan" products do not have any accompanying mark at all. The ceramics are the wares most likely to have had manufacturers' marks. Certain of the better bisque and porcelain pieces, especially the larger figurines, are marked "Andrea" or "Paulux" or with some other name, but it would probably be very difficult to find out today what company these marks represented. Some were cottage industries that have long since disappeared.

The idea of "borrowing" marks from American and European companies was not a new one for the Japanese. They had done it before the war, and *Newsweek* magazine reported, on January 9, 1950, that the Japanese were again "borrowing" marks for their export products. The article accused the Japanese of continuing the practice started before the war, when—it was said—they took advantage of the fact that two Japanese villages were named Usa, thereby giving them a chance to ship crockery to America labeled "Made in USA." The same reporter went on to say that they (the Japanese) "went so far as to change the names of towns to 'Chicago' or other well-known American cities so that they could 'lawfully' slap a 'Made in Chicago' label on their goods."

The biased *Newsweek* reporter claimed that before the war there were "Firezone" tires, "AC" spark plugs, and "Ronson" lighters. Although this practice was watched very closely after the war, inferior-grade lead bearing the brand name "Selby," a product name also used by the American Smelting and Refining Company, was exported from Japan, and Japanese tires bearing the U.S. Rubber Company's trademark "Royal" were shipped to the Philippines. Japanese manufacturers were reported to have applied to their patent office for registration of marks similar to those used by American manufacturers.

The eleven-nation Far Eastern Commission issued a directive in 1950 to ban any deceptive marking on the part of Japanese, and the U.S. Trademark Association put pressure on the State Department to spell out the necessity for stopping the deceptive mark practice in the peace treaty with Japan.

Deceptive marking was, of course, an attempt on the part of Japanese manufacturers to overcome prejudice on the part of American buyers, many of whom boycotted Japanese goods for years following the war. Manufacturers in Japan had not only the resistance of buyers to contend with; they were also constantly being accused by various countries of producing peacetime goods that were copies of products made in those countries or products that were competitive with those of our wartime allies.

Great Britain was the country that complained the most, and there is little doubt that it had good reason. All types of British pottery and porcelain were imitated by the Japanese, and some of the goods were difficult to distinguish from their prototypes.

Some imitations were very bad. The Wedgwood company had sued a Japanese firm in the 1930s to keep it from producing an imitation of the Wedgwood blue and white jasperware and marking it with a mark that was similar to Wedgwood's. The imitation jasperware was again produced during the Occupation, but it has no manufacturer's mark. Since this is one of the least successful Japanese imitations of British pottery, only a novice would confuse it with the real thing.

The only marks the Occupied collector has to be concerned with are the "Made in Occupied Japan" or "Occupied Japan." Since marks on decorative objects are used for dating as well as manufacturer identification, the collector does not really need marks. These collectibles were made only during a period of about five years, and closer dating would be impossible. One manufacturer might have used many different marks to identify different products. Some marks do denote quality merchandise, but others seem to have been used indiscriminately on both excellent and inferior products. The marks illustrated here are merely a sampling of the marks that do exist on Occupied Japan products. Certainly, there are many others.

69. Mark in gold used for lacquer imports. "Occupied Japan" probably did not satisfy customs inspectors, and later imports by same company used "Made in Occupied Japan."

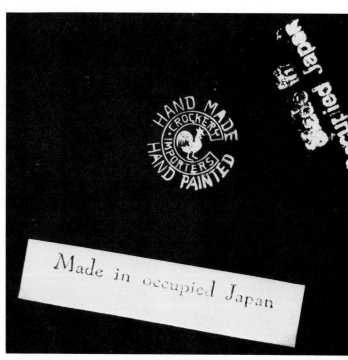

70. A lacquer tray bearing the importer's mark and "Made in Occupied Japan" is stamped in gold; it has a printed paper label as well.

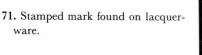

71. Stamped mark found on lacquerware.

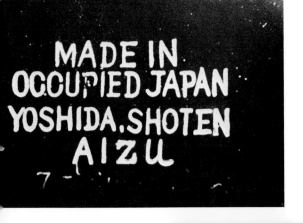

72. Stamped mark found on lacquerware.

73. Stamped mark found on lacquerware.

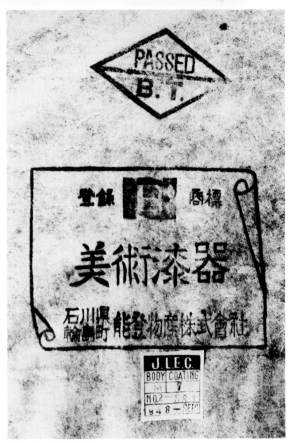

"Occupied Japan" was added to the importer's mark, and "Made in Occupied Japan" was stamped separately. Added to these is the inspector's "OK."

75. Packing box for lacquerware has various stamps and seals.

76. Mark found on lacquered metal relish tray. The paper labels used on some of these pieces are usually missing.

77. Mark from a lacquered metal tra Maker or importer turned the necessa identification mark into a poetic legen "Made by Hand in Occupied Japan."

78. This is the mark most commonly found and the only one that really concerns collectors of Occupied Japan objects. It was embossed, etched, printed under or over the glaze, or stamped, depending on the material of the object.

4

Bisque and Porcelain Figurines

In the production of figurines and figural groups, the Japanese appeared to take literally the first three words of the American Declaration of Independence. A representative group of porcelain and bisque figures marked "Made in Occupied Japan" looks like "We, the People." Replicas of all the races, all age groups, and every national and ethnic group were made. The costumes in which they are dressed range from seventeenth-century style to clothes of the 1930s. Like Noah's ark animals, most of the figurines were made in pairs, although today's collector may find it difficult to match many of the mates.

Porcelain replicas of people have been popular decorations for the home for over two centuries, the best having been made by the Austrians and Germans. In the first half of the eighteenth century, the designer J. J. Kändler set standards for this type of art that have not been reached since his time. There was no real attempt on the part of the Japanese artists and manufacturers to reproduce the painstaking modeling and decorating of the early European figurines. They did make some well-detailed and

79. Both these double figures in porcelain once had mates. Height of the couple at right, 8 inches.

80. Matched pair of porcelain double figurines. Height, 6¼ inches.

81. Double figurines, woman seated, man standing. Predominant color is bright blue. Height, 5½ inches.

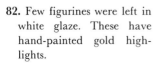

82. Few figurines were left in white glaze. These have hand-painted gold highlights.

hand-painted pieces that were intended to be sold in America's better gift shops and department stores. Since these larger figurines were among the most expensive of all porcelain items marked "Made in Occupied Japan," they are today prime collector's items. Most were made in the last three years of the Occupation, and many of the better ones were used as lamp bases as well as for mantel or shelf decoration.

The most elaborate bisque figural group to have shown up so far is the gondola illustrated in Plate 4. The piece is fifteen inches in height and width, including the two-tier pierced brass base. The bisque part is a fanciful boat with the figure of a woman holding a fan under the canopy while another woman serenades her. A gondolier stands at the opposite end of the boat. Since the piece is better finished on one side, it was obviously meant to be displayed with the other side to the wall. A final touch to this fairytale bisque piece is that it is electrified, and when it is turned on, the base is lighted with a red glow. Although very little that the Japanese made for export during the Occupation was one-of-a-kind, there certainly cannot have been too many of these gondolas made.

83. Seated couple, woman playing mandolin, man playing flute. Height, 3½ inches.

84. Seated musicians. Height, 6 inches.

85. Seated couple.

86. Seated man and woman are "souvenirs of Pine Bush, N.Y." Height, 4 inches.

Charming centerpieces modeled after prewar Austrian and German bisque and glazed porcelain are also highly collectible today. Cherubs pulling or pushing wagons and carts made in the shapes of open flowers are as handsome as their earlier prototypes. These, also, were made in somewhat limited quantity. Eighteenth-century coaches with well-dressed passengers and ladies in sleighs were also made. Some of these were produced in pairs; others were sold separately.

The better bisque figurines were decorated in soft, subtle colors. Some restraint seems to have been used in the application of gold beading and outlining. The faces have character and the drape of the clothing is realistic. In most of the figurines, whether of good quality or not, the hands are the giveaway that defines the pieces as "made in Japan." The fingers are seldom delineated, and on most figurines they do not appear to be naturally shaped.

87. Standing bisque figures in eighteenth-century costume. The woman holds a basket of flowers.

88. Good-quality porcelain figurines. Lady holds a fan. Height, 10 inches.

89. Porcelain figurines. In the woman's hand is an umbrella.

90. Quality porcelain figurines. The man holds his hat in his hand. Predominant color is green.

Pairs of double figural groups in bisque are quite desirable collector's items. These usually identical mirror images were purchased by Americans as mantel decoration. Some charming sets were made, mostly of wooing couples sometimes accompanied by an animal such as a dog or a lamb. Both the rich and poor are represented, and the figures dressed in peasant costume are especially appealing.

Somewhat more plentiful are the single figures that were almost always made in pairs. Many of these are "musical" couples with the suitor playing a lute or some

91. Man with mandolin, woman holding hat.

92. Couple in peasant costume. Height, 8 inches.

other instrument and the woman listening shyly or following the song in a music book. Often the couples, although separate, appear to be dancing with each other. Pairs of seated figures in bisque are rarely found today. They are in high demand if they are the larger, better-quality bisque and marked "Made in Occupied Japan."

Collectors who prefer the shinier glazed porcelain figurines and figural groups of good quality and detail will find that supply has dwindled, as more and more Occupied Japan collectors upgrade their collections. At one time, it was possible to purchase matched pairs of the taller and better-quality figures, but now many collectors settle for single examples even if they are certain that a seated colonial lady with her songbook is listening to the lute of her lover who is miles away in someone else's collection of objects made in Japan during the Occupation.

The glazed figures were made of a more brittle material than the bisque ones and the detailing on the costumes is often better. Ruching and ruffling appear to be almost real and the colors are bright and appealing. When it seemed necessary, the Japanese porcelain makers used a material other than clay for parts of their figurals. One case where this was done is in a small animal and child figurine (see Plate 1). The kneeling child pipes her tune on a tiny metal rod that was inserted into a hole in her mouth. This piece is hand painted but is a more simplified shape than most other "Made in Occupied Japan" figurines.

Although the "Made in Occupied Japan" figurines may not compare in detail or quality with the best European figurines that were made after the war, they do have a great deal of charm, naturalness, and color; and it is important to remember that they were not as expensive as their prototypes when they were new. A pair of good-

93. Bisque figure of peasant woman with deer. Height, 6½ inches.

94. Couple carrying grapes. Man has a basket but the woman holds grapes in her apron. Height, 10¼ inches.

95. Woman in garden party dress is a vision in her porcelain ruffles. Height, 6 inches.

96 A & B. Multiple figural groups are scarce, which is why these two poor-quality porcelain groups are valuable to collectors. **A.** *Joseph P. Valenti;* **B.** *Author's Collection*

97. Scandinavian figurines of fisherman and woman, modeled after Bing and Gröndahl figurines. Color that predominates is blue.

98. Four women figurines in blue and pink.

quality porcelain figurines ten inches in height could be purchased for less than three dollars in American gift shops. The smaller, less detailed pieces sold in novelty stores for only a third that amount. They were a type of useless but decorative item that had not been available during the war years, and so these figurines were popular when new.

99. Musical couple and the original packing box with mark "Made in Occupied Japan."

100 & 101. Two porcelain couples made in the same mold change in appearance when given different color clothing and hair.

102. Porcelain couple made in badly detailed molds.

Period-costumed figurines certainly dominated the Japanese production, but many other types of figurines were made too. Among the most amusing are the many single figures of women dressed in the mode of the 1930s, the last period of Japanese trade with America before the war. Most of these women figurines wear large garden hats and gloves and hold their skirts daintily in their hands. Were it not for the "Made in Occupied Japan" mark, one would insist that the figurines of this type were made during the Art Deco period that disappeared after the start of the war. Bride and groom figures for the tops of wedding cakes can be found that also appear to have been of similar vintage. These were supplied to American bakers for pennies each.

103. Group of "skirt-holders," a style of figurine that was popular in the 1930s.

104. Three women figurines in Art Deco style.

105. Porcelain figures of women holding hat, head, or skirt.

106. Figure of colonial woman; probably she once had a partner for her dance.

107. Woman with dog is in style of the 1930s. Height, 6 inches.

108 A & B. Bride and groom figures in bisque were used on top of wedding cakes during the Occupation years. Those marked "Made in Occupied Japan" are quite scarce.

The catalog page on page 36 shows that many religious figures were produced, both in bisque and in porcelain. Except for the porcelain angels playing musical instruments this illustration yields many surprises for today's collector. This category of "Made in Occupied Japan" figurine has only recently been discovered. It should be of interest for collectors who are willing to pay high prices for the best-quality bisque and porcelain figurines to note that the highest wholesale price on the entire page is twelve dollars a dozen—for the porcelain Madonna and Child (with flower vase). The piece is 6⅛ inches high and at retail would have cost less than two dollars.

Although the Japanese porcelain makers were quite successful in producing products copied from porcelain made elsewhere in the world in just about any type of style, shape, or glaze, there was one type of figurine that sometimes seems to have been beyond their capabilities. These are the figures of ballet dancers on which the Japanese attempted to use a method of porcelain lacemaking that had been perfected by the Austrians and Germans. The process involved dressing a porcelain figure in a real lace costume that was permeated with liquid porcelain and refired. The lace burned away, leaving the lacy fragile pattern in paper-thin porcelain. Through some lack of

RELIGIOUS FIGURES   MADE IN OCCUPIED JAPAN
ALL ITEMS ON THIS PAGE — NET NO DISCOUNT

BP-98142   Doz. .36
Assorted Bisque Figures, in colors and bronze. 2" high.
Packed 1 dozen assorted.

BP-98140   Doz. .60
Assorted Bisque Figures, in colors and bronze. 3¼" high.
Packed 1 dozen assorted.

BP-70559-A   Doz. .73
Praying Child and Angel. Assorted colors. Approximately 3" high.
Packed 1 dozen asst'd. to box.

BP-98516   Doz.
Porcelain Madonna. Colored, gold trim. 2¾" high.
Packed 2 dozen to box.

BP-93433   Doz. .72
Assorted Bisque Figures, in colors and gold. 3½" high.
Packed 1 dozen assorted.

BP-98136   Doz. 1.00
Assorted Bisque Figures, in colors and bronze. 4" high.
Packed 1 dozen assorted.

BP-95470-A   Doz. 1.15
White Porcelain Angel Musicians, trimmed with gold. 2¾" high.
Packed 1 dozen asst'd. to box.

BP-98059-A   Doz. 1.00
Assorted Bisque Figures, in colors and bronze. 3¼" high.
Packed 2 dozen asst'd. to box.

BP-98515   Doz.
Porcelain Madonna and Child. Colored, with gold trim. 2½" high.
Packed 2 dozen to box.

BP-98055-A   Doz. 1.25

Assorted Bisque Figures, in colors and bronze. 5" high.

Packed 1 dozen asst'd. to box.

BP-98138   Doz. 1.10
Bisque Figure. Assorted colors and bronze. 4" high.
Packed 1 dozen asst'd. to box.

BP-98066   Doz.
Bisque Figure. Assorted colors and bronze. 4" high.
Packed 1 dozen asst'd. to box.

BP-98517

Doz. 1.90

Porcelain Figure. Colored, with gold trim. 4¼" high.

Packed 1 dozen to box.

BP-97436   Doz. 2.25
Porcelain Figure. Colored, with gold trim. 5½" high.
Packed 2 dozen to box.

BP-70564

Doz. 4.00

Porcelain Figure. Colored, with gold trim. 5¼" high.

Packed 1 dozen to box.

BP-97674   Doz. 2.40
Bisque Figure. Colored, with gold trim. 6" high.
Packed 1 dozen to box.

BP-98518   Doz. 12.
Porcelain Madonna and Child, with flower vase. Colored, with gold trim. 6⅛" high.
Packed 1 dozen to box.

109 A. Wholesale catalog page from 1950 shows assorted religious figures in bisque and porcelain and gives wholesale prices.

109 B. Photograph of figure advertised at the lower right of page 36, which is a very scarce item for today's collector. *Mr. and Mrs. Frank Forshaw*

110. Girl in period costume with open book.

111. Unusual figure of a cancan dancer with a skirt of porcelainized lace ruffles. Height, 4½ inches.

112. Ballet dancers whose porcelainized lace costumes have not stood up well.

113. Ballet dancers in a variety of rather awkward positions.

understanding of this process or perhaps just to save time and money, the skirts on the Japanese-made ballet dancers were poorly made and seem to have reverted over the years to rather sorry-looking lace, giving the little dancers a somewhat bedraggled appearance.

Because most of the "Made in Occupied Japan" ballet dancers were inexpensive novelty items, they are quite small, ranging from three inches to about five inches. Their features are not as well detailed as those of the larger porcelain figurines and they have a further problem. Evidently, there were few Japanese modelers who understood the positions of classical ballet, and many of the dancers appear in less than graceful stances. The legs on most of them are misshapen and the hands, without delineated fingers, look more like paws. Because so many of these tiny dancers did end

114. The Japanese improved their lacemaking ability in the later figures of ballet dancers produced during the Occupation. The costumes on these three are in good shape.

115. Ballet dancer with skirt made of ruffled porcelain edged in gold. *Author's Collection*

up as children's toys, not too many of them survived and collectors may find it difficult to purchase even a single example today with the "Made in Occupied Japan" mark. Awkward they may be, but rarity on today's market makes them desirable.

Quality and detail in Japanese figurines made during the postwar period seem to vary according to gradations in size. It was easier to get better detail in shape and decoration when the piece was over six or seven inches, and in general the larger figures were of the better quality. An exception is the kneeling child with animals already mentioned. There are figurines of children in comparable size that are not as carefully painted and where the quality of the porcelain and glaze are not comparable.

Although most of the better-quality figurines and figural groups are in eighteenth-century costume, there are some exceptions. A desirable couple are the brightly glazed Siamese dancers shown in Plate 18 and the knight and his lady in Illustration 116. Among the smaller figurines that are not of especially good quality but that

116. A knight and his lady. Predominant color is gray. Height, 10½ inches.

117. Figure of American Indian holding arrows was a souvenir of Washington, D.C. *Author's Collection*

118. Canadian policeman in uniform. *Author's Collection*

appeal to Americans because they were so obviously made for the American market are figures of "Uncle Sam," figurines (Plate 20) of American cowboys and cowgirls, American Indians, and a Canadian policeman.

Ethnic types and figurines in the national costumes of other countries can also be found. These range from Italian organ grinders to Scottish and Dutch couples and single figures. One could specialize only in Oriental figurines and eventually gather an extensive collection of peasants and patricians in just about any age group.

The variety to be found in "Made in Occupied Japan" figurines is so great that it is possible to illustrate only a small portion of the entire production. Certainly, there are hundreds of others that will be found by collectors. Figures of people were used to adorn porcelain bookends, decorate lamps, hold toothpick containers, decorate planters, and as containers for table condiments. Hollow, seated inscrutable Oriental figures were sold in many sizes as incense burners. Certainly, this type of mostly decorative, sometimes useful, porcelain was Japan's most successful export during the period after the war. Other countries of the world may have been able to compete artistically in this type of work, but none could compete as far as price was concerned. A veritable army of Japanese-made porcelain people invaded the North American continent several years after World War II.

119 A. Porcelain figure of an organ grinder with a monkey. **B.** Pottery figures of musicians are copies of German woodcarvings.

120. Pair of Oriental porcelain figures with hats.

121. Pair of porcelain Oriental figurines. Man holds a paint box and brush.

122. Patrician Oriental couple.

123. Kneeling Oriental couple.

124. Pair of peasants with baskets of produce.

125. Girl in pajamas and holding a fan; the man holds a stringed instrument.

126. Small and badly modeled couple. The woman's hair ornaments resemble horns.

127. Siamese dancer and a bust of an Oriental woman.

128. Seated Oriental figures are incense burners. Men on left and right are made from the identical mold but painted differently.

. The reverse side of the incense burners in Illustration 128.

130. Musical couple forever attached to bookends.

131. Oriental figures in porcelain with oversized heads.

132. Young girl on a garden seat.

5

Figural Lamps,
Candleholders, and
Wall Plaques

Perhaps lamp bases marked "Made in Occupied Japan" are the most recently made lighting devices of interest to collectors. Collectors of early lighting devices certainly would have no interest in electric lamps made with porcelain figural bases, and purist collectors who are more interested in art than history would surely search for the French figural lamps that are better made and of a quality of porcelain not attained in even the best of the Japanese copies. Nevertheless, collectors of "Occupied Japan" objects consider the lamps with porcelain figures to be prime collector's items.

Porcelain lamps are difficult to find in pairs today, but it is almost certain that originally almost every "Occupied Japan" lamp base had a partner. The larger figures one finds as shelf ornaments were adapted as lamps, and a familiarity with the better-quality porcelain figural groups will enable the collector to recognize a lamp as being of possible "Occupied Japan" origin. The reason this knowledge is necessary is that most of the figural lamps have metal bases, and so require disassembly before the mark can be found. Lamps made in this way tell their own story. It is fairly obvious

133. Double figures in porcelain are a pair of lamp bases.

134. Musical couple in hand-painted porcelain on a bronzed metal base.

135. The pairs of couples used on these two lamps are not mirror images. The musical instruments were switched.

136. Pair of porcelain lamps. Figurines are doubles and mirror images.

that the figures and bases were imported separately by lamp companies and assembled in the United States.

Lamps that are infinitely easier to identify are those made entirely of porcelain where the mark is clearly seen on the underside. Although the lamps were probably wired in this country, the Japanese molded and decorated the entire base. Where the shades still exist, one can assume that this part of the lamps was imported separately or made in the United States.

137 A. Small single-mold, double-figure lamp base. **B.** Miniature lamp base (height, 6 inches) shows how some lamps were packed with finials and assembled and wired on arrival. **C.** Few porcelain lamps that are not figurals can be found today. This lamp has gold decals and raised flowers. **A.** *Joseph P. Valenti;* **B.** *Author's Collection;* **C.** *Mr. and Mrs. Frank Forshaw*

138. Double figurine lamp was made by mounting a pair of single figures on the same base.

Double figures in mirror images were also made as pairs of lamp bases. Most often, these are Colonial-style figures. Some figures made as man-woman pairs of matching singles were molded together on lamp bases; others were used singly. The lamps in Illustration 139 have metal bases and single figures with predominately blue glaze costume. The molded lamps in Illustration 133 show that the same mold was used; the couple was put together on a single lamp base and the mold reversed so that they form a matching pair of double figured lamps. The costumes are painted in light colors, the skirt of the woman being in a floral pattern. This gives identical figures an entirely different appearance.

Among the most desirable of "Occupied Japan" lamps are the bisque figurals. The work is usually of good quality on the bisque lamps and the colors are soft and subtle. Some of these lamps were made for use in children's rooms, and among the more collectible is a pair of children's figures of a cowboy and cowgirl. These lamps, which have a great deal of charm, are difficult to find since they appeal to many people rather than just to collectors.

139. The porcelain figurines most frequently found are these two in brilliant blue eighteenth-century costumes. The male figure is often called "Blue Boy."

140. Oriental figurine is the base for a lamp and probably was half of a pair.

141. These bisque children figurines are hand painted in pastel colors; mounted on brass bases, they make handsome lamps.

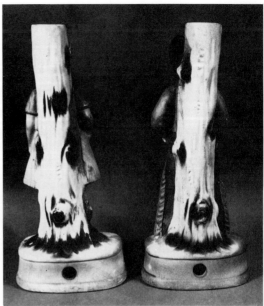

142. Cowboy and cowgirl figurines that were made as lamp bases but never assembled.

143. Reverse of the bisque cowboy and cowgirl lamp figures showing the rustic tree and the hole for the wire.

In comparison to electrified lamps, there are relatively few candlesticks in porcelain marked "Made in Occupied Japan." Those one does find are of a quality leading to the belief that they were made as variety store items rather than gift shop merchandise. Most of those found are double-light candleholders with a figure in the center. The decoration or molding does not compare with that of the figures used as electric lamp bases.

Few pairs of lamps come on the market, but it is probable that many are still in use by the original purchasers. Those who own the metal-based lamps may have no idea that the figures themselves are probably marked "Made in Occupied Japan." Few of these owners realize that collectors search for these pairs of lamps and often are willing to pay high prices for those with exceptional figural pairs of Colonial, Oriental, or Western American themes.

144. Pair of porcelain double figural candleholders.

145. Pair of porcelain double candleholders with musical cherubs. The candleholder in center was once part of a pair also.

Bisque wall plaques were a gift shop item made by the Japanese during the Occupation. Most of these were three-dimensional Colonial figures molded in one operation. All were self-framed and hand colored in soft pastel hues. As is true of many of the figurines, plaques too were made in pairs, with single man-woman figures that face each other, but there were also "couple" plaques, where the man and woman on one plaque match the couple on a companion plaque that is a mirror image of themselves. Because many of the bisque plaques were hung rather precariously, it is easier to find one than it is to acquire a matched pair.

146. Pair of oval bisque wall plaques, hand colored in pastel colors.

147. Bisque wall plaque of a colonial gentleman who once probably had a partner.

6

Figurines of Children

Although the larger Colonial figure groups are the most desirable porcelain for collectors of Occupied Japan, there are thousands of smaller figures that are of equal importance as being representative of the type of object the Japanese made for export. Figures of children were made in great quantity and often sold in sets or pairs. Many of these are only an inch or two in height, and most are representative of European styles in pottery and porcelain.

The Japanese, great borrowers of art styles (as pointed out in an earlier chapter), were able to produce very respectable imitations of the well-known German Hummel figures of children. They also made pottery imitations of German woodcarvings, which are now considered to be worthwhile collector's items. Few of these small figures can be considered works of art, but most of them have great popular appeal, and certain of the sets of children made of porcelain or pottery are especially attractive.

Most of the miniature figures were made for shelf decoration only, but others are

148. Boy and girl figurines.

149. Porcelain figurines of a small girl came packed twenty-four to a carton. Each is marked "Made in Occupied Japan" on the bottom. The box is also marked.

150. Boy and girl bookends; hand-painted porcelain.

151. Boy and girl bookend figurines.

152. Three miniature maidens, all with plant or flower containers.

153. Three juvenile Oriental figures.

attached to small planters or to toothpick or match holders. Others were made into pairs of salt and pepper shakers, and these will be considered in a separate chapter, since there are so many and the variety in shapes is almost limitless.

Angels in a great variety of positions and occupations are one category of collectible miniature figures. Cherubs were made in sets of six as a standing orchestra, with each winged baby playing a different instrument. Tiny musicians, discreetly draped, can be found playing the saxophone, violin, cello, trumpet, drum, or accordion. Each one of a group of shelf-edge seated cherubs also plays a different instrument.

Elves and brownies in a variety of fanciful poses were made too. Many can be found riding insects, butterflies, or shells; the poses for these figures were devised so that they were sitting, lying on their stomachs, or kneeling in very appealing positions. Many of the children were in American cowboy suits, and others, like the larger figures, are dressed in national costumes or period costumes. A few small double figures of cherubs were made.

154 A, B, & C. Good-quality bisque figural planters all have children in period costume as decoration. All are marked "Paulux." **A.** *Author's Collection;* **B & C.** *Joseph P. Valenti*

155 A & B. Cowboy (or girl) on horseback and a miniature coach.

156. Cowboy and cowgirl figurines.

157. Cowgirl in hand-painted bisque.

158. Cowboy resting next to a cactus plant.

159. Cowboy is standing next to a miniature pot intended for use as a toothpick holder.

160. Figure of a black adult and a child playing a concertina.

161. Small bisque figures of child musicians may have been part of a larger musical group.

162. Child musicians in painted porcelain.

163. Pixie musicians.

There are also figures of children dressed in adult-type clothing—small boys in top hats, for instance. A figure of a newsboy is especially charming, as is a small souvenir figure of a boy with his knapsack, who appears to be running away from home. Tiny figures of children in clown outfits can be found in some quantity too.

Although the figures of children were made to sell for a few cents and even the sets of six similar figures were probably available for less than a dollar, the small figurines have strong appeal to collectors. They are presently not very expensive as collector's items, and an enormous variety of them is still to be found. For the collector with limited funds and limited storage space, these tiny people are very desirable. Some are amusing and a few are very carefully made. Perhaps the most wanted of all the children figurines marked "Made in Occupied Japan" are the Hummel types or those small figures made to imitate woodcarvings. Any cowboy or cowgirl figurals are

164. Boy with ice cream cone, boy selling newspapers, and a little boy running away.

165. Motorboat planter was molded in two sections, with the driver being added separately.

166. Clown musicians.

167. Girl with a cat and a boy with a dog.

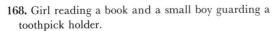

168. Girl reading a book and a small boy guarding a toothpick holder.

also in demand, since they represent an effort on the part of Japanese manufacturers to pander to American buyers by producing subjects that were most familiar.

Unlike the larger porcelain and bisque figures, most of the miniature figures of children were made without much regard for artistic appeal. The figures were mostly

169. A Dutch boy and girl in porcelain are really dinner bells. *Author's Collection*

170. Pairs of cupids draped with grapes.

171. Porcelain cupids on pedestals.

assembly-line products that would find acceptance in variety stores. Decoration was dabbed on in assembly-line fashion, and the porcelain is mainly of poor quality. By law, even these tiny bits of pottery or porcelain had to be marked "Occupied Japan" or "Made in Occupied Japan," and it is seldom that they are found with any additional mark. For collectors who prefer cuteness over quality, there is an almost endless supply of small figural children from which to choose. As in the case of other "Occupied Japan" items, this situation will not prevail much longer as astute collectors continue to purchase all varieties of "Occupied Japan" items.

172. Winged cherub watches over a sleeping infant.

7

Fishbowl Ornaments, Shelf-Edge Sitters, and Porcelain Novelties

In the period just before World War I, it was a fad in the United States to keep a bowl of goldfish; for a while, such fish were probably the most popular of all domestic "pets." The fad probably resulted from the fact that fish were cheaper to buy and feed than most other household pets, and in many American families hit by the Great Depression of the 1930s, they were the parents' substitute when their children begged for a large, expensive animal. Along with the purchase of a glass bowl in which to keep the fish, people usually bought some "Made in Japan" ornaments that would "dress up" the fishbowl.

Many ornaments of this type were produced in Japan during the Occupation— tiny (then very inexpensive) castles, houses, mermaids, coral, and rocks made of bisque or glazed porcelain. These are now desirable collectors' items.

Even more desirable are the figurines of children and animals designed to perch on the rim of the fishbowl. Most of these figures were fishermen (or women), and although it is possible to find them in flea markets, it is seldom that they are found

173 **A & B.** Fishbowl accessories. **A.** *Joseph P. Valenti;* **B.** *Author's Collection*

174. Bisque houses for the bottom of a fishbowl.

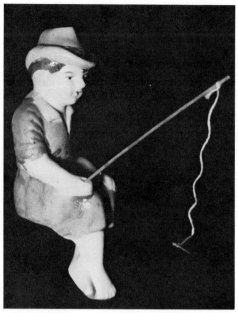

175. Black fisherboy with original bamboo fishing pole, line, and hook. *Sherrill Proctor*

176. Teen-age fisherman holding original striped bamboo fishing pole, line, and hook. Hand-painted bisque. *Author's Collection*

intact. At best, their positions on the glass rim of a bowl were precarious—thousands were made, but many were broken.

Most of today's collectors are unaware of how these bowl-sitters were packed when new. They were packed with a wood block as a seat, so that they could be used as shelf-sitters if one lacked a goldfish bowl on which to perch them. Along with the figurines were packed tiny bamboo-sliver fishing poles with string and hook attached. Most of the wood blocks and bamboo poles have long since disappeared, but the tiny figures make charming shelf-sitters today and are prized by collectors.

Two of the fishermen illustrated here are shown with their original fishing poles; the small black boy in Illustration 175 is perched on the original packing block with wire hook. The teen-age boy in Illustration 176 also holds his original pole. The poles are striped with red, and the fishhooks are positioned high enough over the rim of a fishbowl so that they are not in danger of menacing the innocent goldfish below. The fishpoles held by the remaining ornaments have been improvised.

Although most of the bowl-sitters are young children, a few older figures were made. An unusual figure in bisque is the teen-age couple. Their costume places them in the 1930s, and it is probable that the molds for these figures were made before the war. Unlike other figurines marked "Made in Occupied Japan," not many different molds were made for these. Variety was obtained by using a single figure of a pair. The teen-age boy in Illustration 176 is the identical shape of the boy who has a partner in Illustration 177. Another way to get variety with a minimum of molds was to leave some of the figures in white bisque and to paint costumes on others.

177. Bisque couple sitting on original packing block. *Sherrill Proctor*

Most of the fisher people were made in bisque, but a few can be found in brightly glazed porcelain. The tiny Oriental couple are unusual in this respect, and also because they are a detached pair. Caricatures rather than naturalistic figures, they have brightly painted red, blue, and yellow clothing and glossy black hair.

Menacing cats were made with hooked paws to hang on the outer edge of a fishbowl. These are still being produced, and collectors should check the "Made in Occupied Japan" mark very carefully to make certain that any fishbowl cat is genuinely old. A safer investment would be the green bisque frog illustrated here that was made for the same purpose. The little frog is marked twice—with an impressed mark on its belly and a stamped mark on its feet. Obviously, the manufacturer of this item took no chances that his merchandise would give him any problems with American customs inspectors.

178. Children fishing, in rare unpainted white bisque. *Sherrill Proctor*

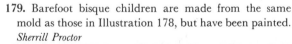

179. Barefoot bisque children are made from the same mold as those in Illustration 178, but have been painted. *Sherrill Proctor*

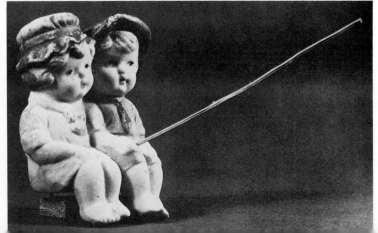

180. Oriental caricature children in porcelain.

181. Green bisque frog made to hang over the edge of a fishbowl.

182. The underside of the frog shows both impressed and printed marks.

Many seated figurines, mainly of children, were made as shelf-edge ornaments. Hundreds of different molds were made for this purpose, and only a few choice examples are illustrated here. Almost all these were made as detached couples and, unlike the fishbowl-sitters, the majority of the shelf-edge ornamental figurines were glazed porcelain rather than bisque. Obviously, many were knocked down and broken over the years; thus, only a small amount of what was originally produced has survived.

All fishbowl ornaments and shelf-edge sitters are now in high demand by collectors. Originally made as inexpensive curiosities, these cute seated children have a special appeal.

Various tiny porcelain novelties and toys were made in Japan during the Occupation for shipment overseas. Some of these are odd or unusual and a few are bizarre.

183. Two pairs of shelf-sitters, a popular novelty item.

184. Oriental shelf-sitters.

Porcelain was molded into the shape of desks, chairs, pianos, organs, suitcases, clocks, lamps, shoes and boots (from cowboy to wooden), and even baby carriages. Miniature furniture was made with and without tiny porcelain occupants. Items in somewhat questionable taste include a match and cigarette holder made in the shape of a clothesline with two sets of underwear hanging on it and a black baby. It is printed with the legend "Who left this behind?"

185 A & B. Miniature porcelain clocks were made in a variety of shapes, colors, and sizes. **A.** *Joseph P. Valenti;* **B.** *Author's Collection*

186. Miniature bowl of fruit.

187. Three items in poor taste were Japanese interpretations of American humor.

188 A & B. Group of footwear in pottery.

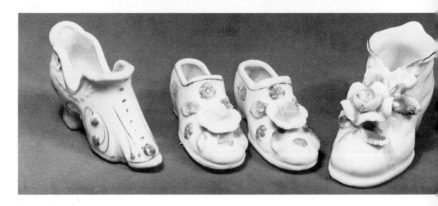

Pieces attempting to appeal to American bathroom humor were made in the shapes of miniature porcelain toilets with wooden lids. These are marked "Ladie's" and "Gent's" by the makers, who were better acquainted with American plumbing than they were with English spelling. Ashtrays with the legend "No Parking" had

189. Three rather peculiar porcelain items.

figurines of a rabbit, a dog, and a red fire hydrant. This is a three-dimensional cartoon that undoubtedly had appeal for some Americans.

Many porcelain boxes were made. Some of these are of poor quality, but others are obviously good-quality gift shop items. Among the worst-made of all Japanese porcelain to come out of the Occupation period is the imitation Wedgwood jasperware. The items were small boxes, vases, and ashtrays. Unlike true Wedgwood, which has applied decoration, the bas-relief is molded into the piece and the designs are not well delineated. The body of this ware is speckled with impurities and is rough and rather crude. The color combinations most often seen are blue on white or white on blue. Were it not for the "Made in Occupied Japan" mark, there would be no reason to own these pieces.

Thousands of miniature tea sets were made in white porcelain with floral decoration. The bulk of these have been lost or broken over the years, and today there are so many collectors of miniatures that the O.J. collector will find strong competition in the marketplace for a set that has remained intact. Very few miniature tea sets were made in glazed pottery without decoration; the one shown in Illustration 195 (at center) is a rarity.

190. White-on-blue imitation Wedgwood jasperware cigarette box.

191. Blue-on-white imitation Wedgwood was poorly made. *Gary Spadoni*

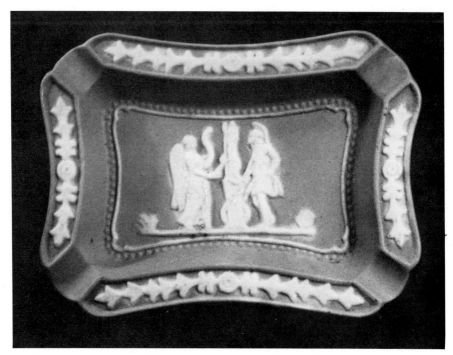

192. Wedgwood-type ashtray, white on blue.

Toothpick holders and tiny boxes were also made in some quantity and in a variety of shapes. Some of the boxes were sold as souvenir pieces—for example, decorated with pictures of Niagara Falls, the Washington Monument, and other places visited by tourists.

Smoking accessories, which included cigarette boxes and urns, ashtrays by the thousands, and match holders, were made in a variety of shapes and styles. Some were decorated in British fashion with three-dimensional flowers.

In general, these small porcelain novelties are not especially well made, although some similar objects can vary in quality. Detail will be better molded and painted on some than on others, and the shapes of some will be more graceful than of others. What the collector must remember is that all miniature novelty items were very inexpensive when new, and were considered "junk" by those people who imported them and sold them. Undoubtedly, they were not regarded as any more important artistically by the Japanese who made them. However, they did have a market in the United States and were made and sold in huge quantities. They were advertised in American wholesalers' catalogs in assortments of twelve dozen at from 65¢ to $1.50 a dozen. Even the storekeeper had no choice of subject in some cases, but that did not matter. The miniature novelties took up shelf space, they were attractive, and the market was good. At retail, none of them sold for more than a half dollar.

The miniature novelty porcelains were early "Occupied Japan" imports that undoubtedly continued to be popular for many years.

IMPORTED PORCELAIN NOVELTIES

0A   **Dozen .65**

lain Novelties. Sizes up to 3½" high. Large variety of best selling items. Exceptional values consisting of Vases, Lamps, Figurines, Pitchers, Dutch ers, Animals, 4 pc. Dog Sets, Clocks, etc. Values up to 25 cents. Each item numbered on box. If you do not want the entire assortment, indicate the ers you prefer, and the amount you wish. Minimum shipment, 12 dozen.   Made in Occupied Japan

25B   **ALL ITEMS ON THIS PAGE — NET NO DISCOUNT**   **Dozen 1.50**

elain Novelties. Sizes up to 5" high. Beautiful assortment of Japanese Larger Figures, Cups and Saucers on stand, Salt & Pepper Shakers, Glass Animal Hand-Painted Italian Pitchers and Vases. Tobe pitchers. Values up to 50 cents. Each item numbered on box. If you do not want the entire assort indicate the numbers you prefer, and the amount you wish. Minimum shipment, 6 dozen.

193. Page from a wholesale catalog of 1950 has illustrations of some of the novelty items made in Occupied Japan.

MINIATURE TEA SETS

BP-92535
Doz. Sets 1.50

Miniature Tea Set on tray. Size of tray, 3". 8 Pieces to set.

Packed 1 dozen sets to box.

BP-98514
Doz. Sets 3.50

Miniature Tea Set on walnut finished stand. Size of stand, 5¼". 9 Pieces to set. Assorted colors and decorations.

Packed 1 dozen assorted sets to box.

194. Catalog advertisement (wholesale) shows the prices of miniature tea sets in 1950.

195. Miniature porcelain tea sets; set in the center is blue-glazed pottery.

196. Tea set and tray in miniature. Cups are ½ inch in height. *Peter Tavera*

197. Miniature teapot, tray, and covered urn; all are painted and gilded porcelain.

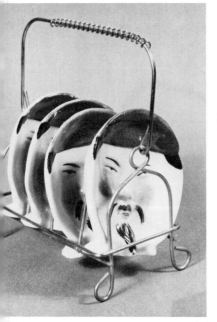

198. Set of ashtrays on a brass wire rack. Oriental faces are molded and painted.

199. Indian profile ashtray.

200. Miniature desk and "swivel" chair have hand lining and pink flower decals.

74

201. Porcelain lamp, sofa with tea-drinking couple, and sofa with couple reading.

202. Miniature porcelain bed and bureau; in the center is a flower-decorated suitcase.

203. Man playing an organ.

204. An organist in miniature.

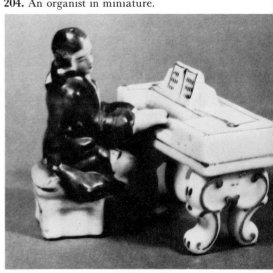

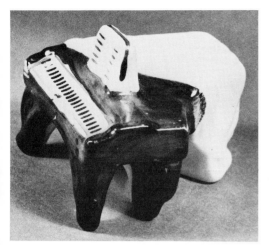

205. Badly molded and painted miniature grand piano. The white portion is supposed to represent a draped scarf.

206. Planter that is the Japanese interpretation of the "Old Woman in the Shoe."

207. Angels playing a concertina adorn both a heart-shaped planter and a circle-of-flowers decoration.

208. Figural wall plaques representing a Dutch family.

8

Animal Collectibles

A vast number of glass, porcelain, and bisque animals were made in Occupied Japan for the novelty and giftware market in the United States and Canada. Many of these were in the forms of planters, toothpick holders, salt and pepper shakers, bookends, and other useful objects; others were novelty figures meant to be purely decorative. They were so inexpensive when new that any American child could gather a collection of dogs or cats on a meager allowance. Hundreds of animal figurines in both realistic and caricature types were made. Some animal figures were stylized in shapes more reminiscent of the 1930s Art Deco period than of the style of the postwar period.

Most of the novelty animal figures were meant to be used as shelf or windowsill ornaments. There were colorful birds, frogs, elephants, cats, squirrels, dogs, horses, rabbits, pigs, and other barnyard animals. Many of these small animals made in glazed porcelain were finished with hand-painted features, an amazing thing considering that the wholesale price of the smaller porcelain figures was less than a dollar a dozen in 1950. The modeling of many of these tiny animal figures is surprisingly good

209. Pigs. *Left:* Shelf ornament. *Center:* Flower - decorated bank. *Right:* Salt shakers.

210. Group of porcelain dogs.

211. Dogs, two with toothache bandages.

212. Bisque dog has baskets for toothpicks attached and is surrounded by more miniature baskets.

213. Pairs of animals, all salt and pepper shakers.

214. The hen in a frying pan, chicks in the nest, and the rooster and scratching hen are all shaker sets.

in view of the original prices for them. Glazes are colorful and the various breeds of dogs are portrayed with realistic coloring and markings.

Many of the animals were made in pairs, often two identical forms, sometimes two figures that are mirror images. Occasionally, there will be a sexual distinction in the pairs—for example, a pecking hen with her preening rooster—that are really salt and pepper shakers. A popular set of shakers was a pair of cartoon-type yellow chicks. These were made also after the Occupation was over, and so collectors should check the marks very carefully. The pair shown here has one genuine and one lacquered-over fake mark.

215. Pelicans, fish, and penguins— all shaker sets.

216. Group of bird shelf ornaments and a penguin bookend.

217. Cute baby birds were popular shakers.

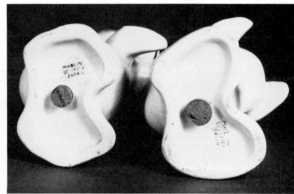

218. The bottom of the shakers in Ill. 217 shows a typical hand-printed fake mark on one and the original stamped mark on the other. On the mark at left, the lacquer coating is obvious.

219. Rooster shelf ornament.

220. Shelf ornament—rabbit and baby.

Although glass and plastic animal figures are scarcer than those made of porcelain and bisque, some were made. Those illustrated in Chapter 16 are from a wholesaler's 1950 catalog, which also lists "Glass Animal Family Sets" consisting of elephants, penguins, ducks, chickens, dogs, and so on, three to five pieces to a set, at the wholesale price of $1.50 a dozen sets. Sizes for these were up to two inches; the glass animals illustrated individually were up to 2½ inches in length. These were all made in assorted colors. The reason they are so difficult to find today is that they were probably marked with a paper sticker rather than embossed with the mark. They were packed one dozen to a box, and the box was undoubtedly marked as well.

The imitation ivory carvings of miniature animals and other figures are also a rarity. These were mounted on black plastic or wood bases; the tiny groups were 73¢ a dozen wholesale. Since very few items were made in plastic during the Occupation, these would be welcome additions to any collection.

221 A. Wide-mouthed frog is an ashtray; good-quality porcelain in brown and white glaze. **B.** Pipe-smoking frog pair are salt and pepper shakers. **A.** *G. Bradley Rainer;* **B.** *Joseph P. Valenti*

222. A stylized pony bank has pink and blue spots.

Although most of the novelty animal figures are still available in some quantity, there are so many collectors of a single type of animal that "Occupied Japan" collectors will find they have some competition for the more popular types of porcelain pets. Frogs seem to be especially scarce in spite of the large number made.

223. "Three Little Pigs" is a tiny shelf ornament.

224 A & B. "Speak, see, and hear no evil" monkey group and three monkey musicians.

225. Pottery elephants make a planter and a cigarette box with ashtray lid.

226. Elephant planters and a shelf ornament.

227. Pottery horses are bookends.

9

Chinaware

Before the war, the Japanese manufacturers of tableware, both porcelain and pottery, had enjoyed a lucrative market abroad, and so it was natural that this trade should be resumed as soon after the war as circumstances and General MacArthur would permit. American bombs had devastated most of the large factories in Japan. The Noritake firm, the only chinaware producer that had not been converted to the manufacture of other wartime products, had received some damage but remained in business throughout the war. Other chinaware makers had to retool and reorganize. Most of them had to start from scratch.

Noritake, originally founded for the purpose of making chinaware solely for export, began its business in 1876 when the Morimura brothers opened an office in New York to facilitate the importing of Japanese porcelain into the United States. By 1904 Noritake opened a large manufacturing complex in Nagoya, where it produced all products necessary for the making of chinaware. The company became the leader in its field. At the beginning of this century, there was a rage in the United States for

228. Part of tea set made in Western style and marked "Noritake."

all things Japanese, and there are many American collectors today who still revere the paper-thin porcelain that was sent over.

Certain Oriental patterns were familiar to most Americans because of the great number of tea sets, luncheon sets, dessert sets, and the amount of other tableware that had been made long before the war. Along with these, Noritake had also made dishes to please Western taste, with some patterns and shapes adapted from English, French, German, and Italian china.

Because of the necessity to resume trade after the war as quickly as possible, there was very little innovative porcelain or pottery sent from Japan at that time. Since the Occupation, the Japanese porcelain and pottery industry has become a world leader in innovative designs for tableware, but the "Made in Occupied Japan" collector of chinaware will find that the shapes and patterns of china dishes made during the

229. Pieces from a tea set made in a style to suit American customers.

short period after the war strongly resemble all the types made earlier in this century. In many cases, quality was abandoned for quick markets and low prices, in order to facilitate financial recovery in as short a time as possible.

Some of the traditional patterns that had had a steady market prior to the war were produced in such quantity that it appeared almost as if there had been no interruption in their manufacture. Because the United States had never been a great producer of ceramic tableware, there was a need for sets of dishes—the demand was strong enough to overcome the prejudice that prevailed among many Americans during the Occupation against purchasing Japanese products.

By 1950, however, certain of these traditional Japanese patterns and shapes in dishes began to look a little old-fashioned and out of style. The porcelain plates with luster borders were reminiscent of the 1920s and 1930s. Dragons and teahouses were no longer fashionable motifs for cups and saucers. Therefore, the Japanese seem to have concentrated on making dishes in any of the traditional shapes and patterns of the world except their own. Today, Satsuma-style dishes with heavy gilding, dishes with hand-painted scenes of Japan, blue and white allover patterns, and other types of dishes made in prewar Japan are very desirable and collectible. Those made during the Occupation in limited amounts are also in great demand. The quality of traditional Japanese patterns made during this period will vary from very fine to terrible.

Those collectors of "Occupied Japan" chinaware who look for quality pieces may search for a long time before they will find a complete tea set or dinner set marked with both the Noritake mark and the "Made in Occupied Japan" mark. Although Noritake undoubtedly made the bulk of the porcelain that was shipped here after the war, they did not use their trademark on much of it. Their mark had long been known for quality, and a lot of what was produced was not felt to be worthy of the

230. Unusual tea set made from molds used before the war. Among the pieces is a flower vase. The dragons are brown with heavy raised white dots.

231. Cake plate with rose decoration is marked "Gold Castle/Made in Occupied Japan."

232. Place plate in dark red with gold. The center motif is decalcomania. *Cookie Bartosewicz*

trademark. Some Noritake pieces were marked with the initials "R.C." for Rose China, and there is little doubt that a variety of other marks were used as well. Undoubtedly, it was thought to be better business if marks were devised that at first glance would mislead a customer in the United States into thinking the china had been made in England. The "Made in Occupied Japan" was often printed in very small letters that were incorporated into the design of the mark.

A few of the chinaware and pottery patterns were so familiar to Western customers that it was like seeing old friends again. Perhaps the most familiar pattern of tableware to arrive during the Occupation was the blue and white Willow pattern that had not lost its popularity in America through two centuries. The pattern was originally designed in China, and George Washington had owned a set in this style. English potters adapted the pattern early. It has remained so popular that it is still being made by both the Japanese and the British.

The Willow pattern was a staple the Japanese potters knew had a good market in the United States, and they were able to produce it in a heavy serviceable quality for kitchen use and for restaurants and diners. Prices for this attractive printed pattern were so low during the Occupation that the Japanese had no trouble competing in the United States market. A 38-piece dinner set was nine dollars at wholesale, and a 17-piece tea set only $3.25. Partitioned grille plates for restaurants were under six dollars a dozen. Willowware eggcups and even doll dishes with the "Made in Occupied Japan" mark can be found, but the pattern will vary in quality.

Of the better types of chinaware made during the Occupation, much is Western in style and less is traditionally Oriental. The Satsuma tea set illustrated in Plate 22

CROCKERY AND GLASSWARE — MADE IN OCCUPIED JAPAN

ALL ITEMS ON THIS PAGE — NET NO DISCOUNT

WILLOW WARE

WILLOW WARE
3 PARTITION BLUE PLATE

71   Case lots   Set 3.25   BP-91169   Case lots   Set 6.75
Less than case lots   Set 3.50   Less than case lots   Set 7.50

Tea Sets in Blue Willow Design consisting of: 32 piece Luncheon Set in Blue Willow Design consisting of:
and 6 Saucers   1 Sugar Bowl with Cover   6 Cups and 6 Saucers   6 Bread and Butter Plates 6"
r   1 Teapot with Cover   6 Dessert Dishes   1 Platter 12"
Packed 1 set to carton, 24 sets to case.   6 9" Dinner Plates   1 Baker 10"
Packed 1 set to carton, 12 sets to case.

-92622   Case lots   Set 9.00   Less than case lots   Set 9.60

piece Dinner Set in Blue Willow Design consisting of:
ups and 6 Saucers   6 Dessert Dishes 5"   1 Baker 16"
inner Plates 9½"   6 Bread and Butter Plates 6"   1 Platter 12"
up Plates 9"   Packed 1 set to carton, 8 sets to case.

BP-91534   Case lots   Doz. 5.40
Less than case lots   Doz. 6.00

10½" Three Partition Plate, Blue Willow Design. For home and restaurant use.

Packed 1 dozen to carton, 10 dozen to case.

233. Catalog advertisement for blue and white Willow ware. Prices (1950) are wholesale.

234. Grille plate is heavy and durable; it was used in restaurants and diners.

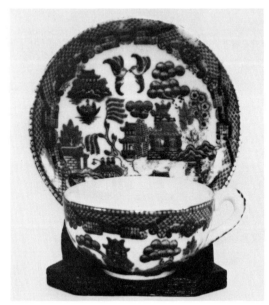

236. Egg cups in Willow pattern were sold separately. *Rachel Valenti*

235. Miniature cup and saucer show that the blue transfer pattern was not carefully applied.

is a good-quality porcelain with decoration that is carefully painted and heavily gilded for American taste. It is marked "Sone China." Collectors will find Satsuma-style cups and saucers that are very badly decorated, although the general appearance is close to that of the "Sone" tea set.

The gold luster tea set shown in Plate 33 and Illustration 238 was made at the end of the Occupation, and much can be deduced about its history from the decoration and marks. The porcelain is of excellent quality, pure white in color. The cups, saucers, and cake plates are hand painted, with each group of three pieces painted with matching flowers. The painting was obviously done in the United States by an artist who was not quite professional at the art of china painting. Nevertheless, the overglaze decoration is attractive and colorful.

237. Satsuma-type cup and saucer.

238. Luncheon plates, cups, saucers, and salt and pepper set are part of a tea service painted in the United States on Japanese blanks. All pieces are marked "Made in Occupied Japan" in acid etching on an unglazed panel. Plates are lustered, gilded, and painted overglaze with a variety of flowers.

Plate 1. Figurine of a small girl charming woodland animals with music from a flute. Height, 4 inches. *Author's Collection.*

Plate 2. Red lacquer finger bowl and plate. There is a gold inlay design on the bowl, which was part of a six-piece set. Diameter of the bowl, 5 inches; height, 2½ inches. Plate (*right*) has a leaf design in gold inlay and a raised floral design in buff lacquer. Diameter, 6⅞ inches.

Plate 3. Porcelain centerpiece with a sleighing couple in Russian costume.

Plate 4. Bisque gondola on pierced brass double-tier base. Marked on the bottom of the bisque is "Maruyama." Extremely rare. Height and length, 15 inches.

Plate 5. Bisque centerpiece—a cherub pulling a cart. Raised dots, gilding, and three-dimensional roses decorate the cart. Length, 7½ inches.

Plate 6. Bisque centerpiece of a child pushing a cart. Marked "Paulux." Height, 4½ inches.

Plate 8. Pair of double bisque figure groups of couples with lamb. Marked "Andrea." Height, 4½ inches.

Plate 7. Figurine of a cherub working at an anvil. Finished cross lies at the rear. Height, 4¾ inches.

Plate 9. Pair of hand-painted seated bisque figures. Height, 5 inches.

Plate 10. Hand-painted bisque figurine of a woman with a lamb on her shoulder. There is raised gold beading on the dress. Marked "Paulux." Height, 7¾ inches.

Plate 11. Bisque figure of a woman in eighteenth-century costume. Marked "Royal Sealy." Height, 9¼ inches.

Plate 13. Bisque three-dimensional wall plaques, self-framed, of Colonial couple in a garden.

Plate 12. Bisque figural group represents a wooing couple with a dog. Height, 6 inches.

Plate 14. Porcelain centerpiece with a coach, horses, and a woman passenger. A man walks alongside. Marked "Ulux." Length, 8½ inches.

Plate 15. Pair of porcelain figural groups with a man pushing a woman in a sleigh; a spotted dog is beside the man. Length, 8 inches.

Plate 16. Pair of porcelain figurines with exceptional modeling and detail; hand-painted and gilded.

Plate 17. Seated woman with an open book; also a wooing couple. Figure at left is 5 inches high. Both are marked "Maruyama."

Plate 18. Pair of Siamese dancers with exceptional color and detail.

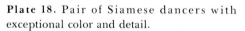

Plate 19. Toby mug of General MacArthur.

Plate 20. "Uncle Sam" figures. Height, 4 inches and 6½ inches.

Plate 21. Group of three toby mugs in a style "borrowed" from the British potters.

Plate 22. Part of a tea set in Satsuma style. The porcelain is exceptionally good quality, and the decoration is skillfully applied. Marked "Sone China."

Plate 23. Gold-coated cordial set, hand-painted. Tray, 7 inches in diameter.

Plate 24. Group of children figurines in porcelain. The style of the modeling was adapted from Hummel figures.

Plate 25. Group of pottery figures of old men in a style adapted from German woodcarvings.

Plate 26. Elves and brownies riding on insect shells, and butterflies were popular she ornaments.

Plate 27. Black musicians were made in sever sizes and were sold separately or in group

Plate 28. Figurines of two ancient Chinese men.

Plate 29. Oriental figures carrying salt and pepper shakers. At left, baskets of produce hang from the yoke. The figure at right carries pigs in baskets.

Plate 30. A plate of good-quality porcelain bearing a scene with a pagoda and other buildings along a river-bank.

ate 31. Plates in Chinese style with plum blossom coration and luster borders.

Plate 32. Cups and saucers with slip-trailed dragons and airbrush designs are of a style made before the war, but all the pieces shown are marked "Made in Occupied Japan."

e 33. Serving pieces of a tea set with gilding hand decoration done in the United States. All pieces except the cake plate are marked "Made Occupied Japan." The cake plate is marked de in Western Zone Germany"!

Plate 34. Kaga-style cup and saucer in soft pastel colors are good-quality porcelain. Marked "Made in Occupied Japan."

Plate 35. Blue and white Willow pattern in heavy porcelain was popular in the United States and sold well. This set was made up of pieces that included both prewar and postwar stock. Later pieces in this pattern were not as good quality. The large piece is marked "Made in Japan/Occupide." The piece was obviously refired so that "Occupide" could be added to mark.

Plate 36. Two salt and pepper sets. In each set, the top part lifts off, and the base part (the drum or the rock) is the second shaker. The rock is marked Robin Hood.

Plate 37. Pair of hand-painted black lacquer vases. Height, 9 inches.

Plate 38. Teacups and saucers, gold lacquer with hand-painted decoration.

The heavily gilded pieces are marked in an unglazed panel on the back with the words "Made in Occupied Japan" acid etched in script. The mark can be detected only when the pieces are held at just the right angle. One piece is initialed over the glaze by the artist-decorator, and the date 1953 appears on one of the pieces. There is one interesting exception to these marks, however. The large cake platter, which appears to match the rest of the set and is decorated with a spray of pink roses, has the same size unglazed panel on the reverse side. However, when this piece is held at the proper angle to the light, one can read "Made in Western Germany." This tea set, evidently a fiftieth anniversary gift, represents some interesting postwar history

2556
lots   Doz. 2.25
than case lots
            Doz. 2.40
Demi-Tasse Cup and
Medium weight, 2¼"
Multi-colored decora-

ked 2 dozen to box,
8 dozen to case.

BP-92485
Case lots   Doz. 2.40
Less than case lots
                Doz. 2.65
Chine Demi-Tasse Cup and
Saucer. Fine lightweight
china, 2¼" high. Iridescent
finish, two tone color, floral
decorations.

Packed 2 dozen to box,
48 dozen to case.

BP-92389
Case lots   Doz. 3.25
Less than case lots
                Doz. 3.60
Fine China Demi-Tasse Cup
and Saucer. 2¼" high.
Footed cup, delicate floral
decorations.

Packed 2 dozen to box,
48 dozen to case.

239. Advertisement in a 1950 wholesale catalog for demitasse cups and saucers.

240. Six cups and saucers on a gilt metal rack.
Author's Collection

241. Rack with six cups and saucers in kelly green, with tiger lilies and tulips.

242 **A & B.** Porcelain miniature
demitasse cups and saucers in an
unusual square shape. **A.** *Joseph
P. Valenti;* **B.** *Author's Collection*

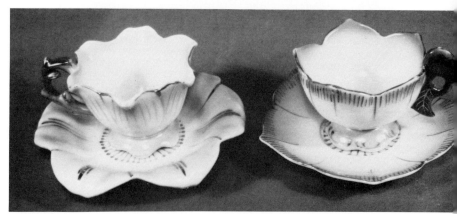

243. Demitasse cups and saucers in floral shapes.

244. The cup at left is in a design "borrowed" from an Italian pattern.

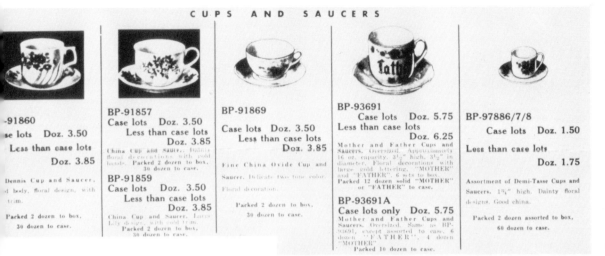

CUPS AND SAUCERS

-91860	BP-91857	BP-91869	BP-93691	BP-97886/7/8
se lots Doz. 3.50	Case lots Doz. 3.50	Case lots Doz. 3.50	Case lots Doz. 5.75	Case lots Doz. 1.50
Less than case lots	Less than case lots	Less than case lots	Less than case lots	
Doz. 3.85	Doz. 3.85	Doz. 3.85	Doz. 6.25	Less than case lots
				Doz. 1.75

245. Catalog advertisement for "Made in Occupied Japan" cups and saucers.

By far the greatest amount of chinaware made during the Occupation for export was in the shape of cups and saucers. These were sold singly, often with a display stand, or in sets of four or, more often, six. A popular gift set included a metal stand that held six demitasse cups and saucers. Cups and saucers in every conceivable shape and style were made to be used as shelf or cabinet display pieces. Floral shapes were popular, and cups and saucers with hand-painted flowers and bright, somewhat garish background colors were made by the thousands. Oversize "Mother" and "Father" cups were a popular item too. By far the greatest number of cups and saucers made were copies of English bone china sets of the type sold as souvenir pieces. Others were knock-offs of continental styles ranging from Delft to Capo-di-Monte.

Because they are in short supply, the most desirable of all cups and saucers marked "Made in Occupied Japan" are those made in the traditional Japanese patterns. Cups with heavy decoration of slip-trailed dragons and luster interiors are difficult to find, as are those decorated with Japanese buildings, people, and scenery. Many collectors specialize in just one size cup and saucer, the miniatures being the most desirable.

246. Cups and saucers with colonial printed design were adapted from English bone china.

247. Teacups and saucers edged in bright colors, with floral prints in the centers.

248. Porcelain teacups with floral borders.

CUPS AND SAUCERS ON STAND

BP-91836   Doz. 1.50

Miniature Cup and Saucer on wood stand. Size of saucer, 1¾". Beautifully decorated.

Packed 1 dozen assorted to box.

BP-71064   Doz. 2.00

Miniature Porcelain Demi-Tasse Cup and Saucer on a walnut finished stand. Size of saucer, 3". Exquisite decorations and shapes.

Packed 1 dozen assorted to box.

BP-98520   Doz. 6.00

Standard Size Footed Demi-Tasse Cup and Saucer on a mahogany finished wood stand. Transparent china, with exquisite gold decorations. Individually boxed.

Packed 1 dozen to box.

249. Catalog advertisement showing cup and saucer sets merchandised with stands.

250. Miniature cups and saucers shown on their original wooden stands.

251. Porcelain sweetmeat box with gold border and three-dimensional flower decoration.

252. Porcelain candy dishes in shell and leaf shapes.

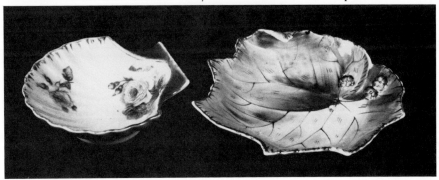

Complete dinner sets, luncheon sets, demitasse sets, and tea sets are somewhat difficult to find today. The fine porcelain pieces are especially scarce, but the heavier Willowware pieces were made to be serviceable and so were often chipped, broken, and thrown away. Nevertheless, there is still a large enough supply of individual china pieces marked "Made in Occupied Japan" for this to become a fascinating category to collect.

10

Kitchen Pottery

It is in the area of kitchen pottery that we find a really enormous variety of techniques and subject matter used by the Japanese potters. They had an ability to adapt styles, shapes, glazes, colors, and motifs from almost any other potter in the world. Cottage pottery made in Staffordshire, England, was so faithfully copied that, were it not for the "Occupied Japan" mark on each piece, any expert would be hard put to identify the pieces as Japanese. "Ye Olde Fireside" is not exactly a Japanese subject for a teapot.

Fruit and vegetable shapes are numerous in salt and pepper shakers, tea sets, and covered jars. A rather heavy version of Irish Belleek was made into shakers and jars as well. Some of the copies of European pottery were not as successful as others, but on the whole the Japanese kitchen pottery is a fascinating category of collectible if one realizes that the variety is endless and the original cost of these items was so low that it made these imitations of more expensive pottery available to everyone.

By far the largest single category for collecting within the larger area of kitchen

253. Back view of "Ye Olde Fireside" teapot. This heavily glazed pottery piece is a design adapted from Staffordshire ware.

254. Strawberry creamer and sugar bowl on a leaf-pattern tray; tomato-shaped cookie jar.

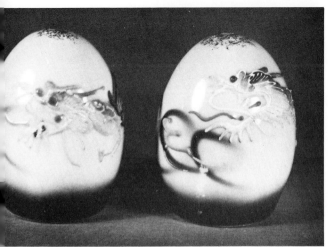

255. Egg-shaped salt and pepper set has an airbrushed design with slip-trailed dragons.

Teapots — Tea Sets — Beer Mugs — Vacuum Bottles—Made in Occupied Japan
ALL ITEMS ON THIS PAGE — NET NO DISCOUNT

ROCKINGHAM WARE TEAPOTS

BP-91595
Case lots   Doz. 2.25
Less than case lots   Doz. 2.50
Tea Pot. 1½ Cup. Plain, undecorated.
Packed 24 dozen to case.

BP-90987
Case lots   Doz. 2.75
Less than case lots   Doz. 3.00
Tea Pot. 2 Cup. Plain, undecorated.
Packed 12 dozen to case.

BP-91240
Case lots   Doz. 3.75
Less than case lots   Doz. 4.00
Tea Pot. 2 Cup. Handsomely decorated.
Packed 12 dozen to case.

BP-90955
Case lots   Doz. 6.50
Less than case lots   Doz. 7.20
Tea Pot. 4 Cup. Handsomely decorated.
Packed 10 dozen to case.

BP-96667A
Case lots   Doz. 10.80
Less than case lots   Doz. 11.40
Tea Pot. 6 Cup. Decorated with raised multi-colored floral design, trimmed with gold. Three styles: fluted, hexagon and round.
Packed 6 dozen assorted styles to case.

BP-91596
Case lots   Doz. 2.40
Less than case lots   Doz. 2.65
Individual Tea or Coffee Pot. 1½ Cup. Plain, undecorated.
Packed 24 dozen to case.

BP-95067
Case lots Doz. 9.60
Less than case lots Doz. 10.80
Tea Pot. Full 5 Cup. Raised floral pattern in light cream color.
Packed 6 dozen to case.

TEA SET

BP-95480
Case lots   Doz. Sets 9.00
Less than case lots   Doz. Sets 10.00
Tea Set. Consists of Sugar, Creamer, and Tea Pot. Beautiful Dutch design. Exquisite coloring. Tea Pot, 4" in diameter, approximately 4½" high. Each set individually boxed.   Packed 8 dozen to case.

SUGAR AND CREAMER SET

BP-92463
Case lots   Doz. Sets 6.00
Less than case lots   Doz. Sets 6.75
Sugar and Creamer Set. Beehive shape, in lustrous cream corrugations with orange and brown bees. Creamer, 2¾" high, 3⅜" at base. Each set individually boxed.   Packed 15 dozen to case.

BEER STEIN

BP-96465
Case lots   Doz. 4.80
Less than case lots   Doz. 5.25
Beer Stein. Beautifully colored. 6" high.
Packed 1 dozen to carton, 12 dozen to case.

PORCELAIN CIGARETTE BOX

BP-93401   Doz. 4.50
Porcelain Cigarette Box, with Ash Tray base. 4" high. Assorted colors.
Packed 1 dozen assorted colors to box.

BEER MUGS

BP-92518
Case lots   Doz.
Less than case lots   Doz.
Beer Mug. Two tone light and brown earthenware. Beautiful designs. 4" high.
Packed 1 dozen to carton, 30 dozen to case.

BP-92519
Case lots   Doz.
Less than case lots   Doz.
Beer Mug. Same as BP-92518. high. Packed 1 dozen to case. 20 dozen to case.

BP-95340
Case lots   Doz.
Less than case lots   Doz.
Beer Mug. Barrel Shaped. Two light and dark brown earthenware. 4" high. Packed 1 dozen to case. 18 dozen to case.

VACUUM BOTTLE

BP-11224 Case lots   Each
Less than case lots   Each
Pint Vacuum Bottle, with Red Pouring Spout and White Stopper. Enameled steel corrugated body. Spring shock absorber, nickel plated cup and shoulder in a corrugated box.
Packed 100 pieces to case.

BP-53374
Case lots   Each
Less than case lots   Each
Quart Vacuum Bottle. Same as 11224. Each in a corrugated box.
Packed 72 pieces to case.

256. Catalog page, New York Merchandise Company, 1950, illustrating various items of kitchenware and the wholesale prices charged for them.

257 A. Shaker sets in a style adapted from Irish Belleek. On the left is a pair of bees; at center is a tray with shakers and a mustard jar; at right is a shaker set in a double basket. **B.** Bee characters were used as shelf figures as well as shakers. Here are four bee musicians.

258. Pitcher in beehive style was adapted from Belleek.

pottery is the salt and pepper shaker set. These were made in so many shapes, motifs, colors, and sizes that one must have respect for the unlimited imagination of the artists who designed them. The quality of both the pottery and the decoration will vary from very good to terrible, but since these were items that originally sold for little more than a quarter when they were new, it is surprising that so much effort was used to vary the styles and that such a huge variety was produced.

Salt and pepper shakers were made in almost any possible imaginable shape—children, animals, fruit, vegetables, buildings, boats, flowers, plants, birds, teapots, coffeepots, and insects, to name only a few. Frequently, three- or four-piece sets were made with a holder and mustard jar added to the salt and pepper shaker. All four

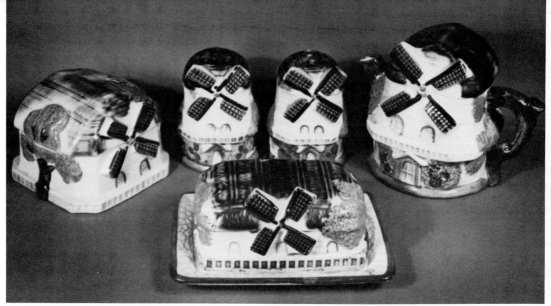

259. Delft-style mustard pot, shaker set, teapot, and butter or cheese dish.

pieces would be integrated into a single design such as a gondola, a canoe, or a house. Human figures in great number and in a variety of national costumes and poses were also used as designs for shakers.

Although pottery is the material used most often for shaker sets, there are also

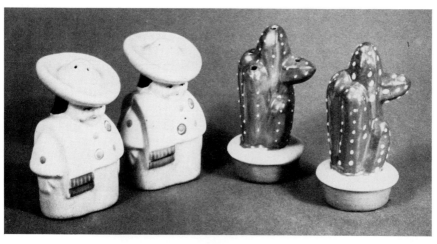

260. Shaker sets in shape of Mexican ures and cactuses.

261. Shaker sets v butterflies.

262. The Dutch girl's extended skirts hold a mustard pot and salt and pepper shakers.

263 & 264. Figural shaker sets represented nearly every nation of the world.

265. Pottery holder with yellow plastic shakers. The use of plastic in Occupied Japan items was rare.

266 A. Three-piece shaker set of black boy holding watermelon slices. **B.** Porter carrying suitcases, which are really salt and pepper shakers.

267. Group of shaker sets with a set in Humpty Dumpty shape in the center.

268. Shaker sets. The center of the canoe is a mustard jar.

269. Gondola shaker set and a pair of shakers in the style of toby mugs.

some very good porcelain ones. Perhaps the set most in demand is the one illustrated in this chapter, of porcelain with decal portraits of George and Martha Washington as decoration. Other American patriotic or regional themes that show up in salt and pepper sets are figural busts of American Indians, either shown realistically or in cartoon style.

270. Delft-style shaker sets with a Dutch boy and girl set in the center.

271. Porcelain salt and pepper shakers.

272. Porcelain shakers with decal portraits of George and Martha Washington are desirable collector's items.

Perhaps the most difficult salt and pepper sets to find intact today are those that have rather precarious designs. Obviously, many of these broke. It is difficult not to break a saltshaker in the shape of a basket hanging on the yoke of a carrier by a string. Basket-shaped shakers of pottery that are held in either hand of an Oriental figure were easily knocked off and broken. Two scarce shaker sets (see plate 36) for which collectors search are the dancing bear on a drum, which—if separated— might never be put back together again; another scarce item is the Robin Hood figure on a rock. The variety of shapes, glazes, and designs in salt and pepper kitchen and table sets is almost endless. Very few are marked with anything except the all-impor- tant "Made in Occupied Japan" stamp.

A great many items besides shaker sets were made in kitchen pottery. Tea sets and teapots were made in some quantity. The desirable items in this category are the

273, 274, 275. Just a few of the shaker sets marked "Made in Occupied Ja- pan" in the shape of fruit and vegetables.

cottage tea sets fashioned after English versions. These house designs are charming, and all are somewhat difficult to find today. Especially scarce items in this category are the cheese or butter dish illustrated here and the salt, pepper, and mustard set that includes an underdish. Tea sets in vegetable shapes were also made, but the quality of these items is not as good as of other cottage pottery. Tomatoes and strawberries are the shapes most frequently seen in this type of ware.

276. Porcelain shaker and mustard set and a candy dish.

277. Rockingham teapot, styled after an English prototype, is marked "Made in Occupied Japan."

278. Six pieces of pottery go together to form a cottage—saltshaker, pepper shaker, mustard pot with lid and spoon, and a tray.

279. Rare cheese dish or butter dish in "Ye Olde Fireside" design to match a tea set. (See teapot in Ill. 253.)

Match holders, spoon trays, and other odds and ends for the kitchen can be collected. All pottery with an American theme is of interest to collectors. One type of figural salt and pepper shaker that is peculiar and collected only because it would never be made today is the black-face stereotype of the male and female cooks. Although the prejudice that these "Uncle Remus" and "Aunt Jemima" figures represent should have been distasteful to both the Japanese makers and their American customers, they are designs found too frequently in "Occupied Japan" novelty items. Fortunately, they are no longer made today, and collectors who realize this are putting away all the black figures they can find. They represent an unfortunate part of America's past, and as collector's items, they remind us of an era that will never repeat itself.

The huge variety of forms to be found in pottery kitchen items made by the Japanese for American use after World War II is remarkable. These were items made to sell for pennies when they were new. Many were types that had been produced before the war, and probably they were made from old molds that still existed. Others were new designs that would appeal to the American housewives who collected salt and pepper shakers as novelty items and for kitchen decoration rather than use. There are still thousands of American women who have substantial collections of salt and

280. Pottery mustard pot in the shape of an old potbellied stove.

281 **A.** "Americana" figurals are very popular with collectors. These black cooks are souvenirs of Niagara Falls. **B.** Baseball salt and pepper shakers are a rarity. **A.** *Joseph P. Valenti;* **B.** *Author's Collection*

pepper shakers who are unaware that those sets marked "Made in Occupied Japan" have more than passing value to many new collectors.

A "Made in Occupied Japan" collectible that only a few years ago was available in some abundance but has recently become scarce is the replica of the German beer stein. In the same category can be grouped the copies of English toby mugs and pitchers. The portrait, or toby, mug that is most in demand because it is, perhaps, the most representative of the time in which it was made and the circumstances under which it was produced is a portrait mug of General Douglas MacArthur.

Most of the mugs were copies of German or English prototypes. Others were adaptations. One blue and brown glazed pottery mug appears to be of German make until it is examined closely and the motifs are recognized as American cowboy symbols. The cowboys appear again on barrel-shaped mugs that have figural handles of acrobatic cowboys. In an effort to cater to American taste, the Japanese also made some mugs with figural handles of nude women. In general, it must be said that the pottery mugs are of questionable quality and workmanship. However, they are col-

282. Pottery toby mugs and pitcher *(center).*

283. Beer mugs. The one at left has a Western motif—cowboy hat and gloves.

284. Pottery beer mugs in styles copied from German and English potters.

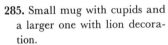

285. Small mug with cupids and a larger one with lion decoration.

286. Pottery mugs with figural handles. The one at right is a surprised cowboy.

287, 288. Pottery toby mugs.

orful, many are hand painted, and a few are rather good copies. Some are amusing in that a very English or German style of modeling is painted with what appear to be Oriental features. Both the toby mugs and the beer steins were dime-store items that were sold for three or four dollars a dozen wholesale.

11

Vases and Planters

Nobody needs to be reminded that the Japanese love flowers and that the art of flower arranging is closely tied to the Japanese reverence for nature and natural forms. The national art of flower arranging has, for centuries, required special pottery flower containers, which the Japanese pass on from generation to generation. These containers are usually low-rimmed dishes that are undecorated except for fine glazes, so that they will not compete with the beauty of the flowers but will complement it. Cylindrical tall vases are also used for many types of arrangements.

Unfortunately, only a few of this type of vase or pottery dish were made during the Occupation for shipment to the United States. Of the great many vases and flower containers marked "Made in Occupied Japan," most are the overdecorated porcelain or pottery of the type that the Japanese knew from previous experience would find a ready market in the West. Few of these are adaptable as flower containers. An exception is a cylindrical vase ten inches tall, hand crafted of unglazed buff-colored pottery. It is decorated in contemporary style of the early 1950s, with a coral band outlined in

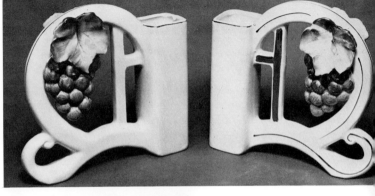

289. Pair of bud vases with grape ornament.

290. Flower pots decorated in the style of Italian pottery.

black. The "Made in Occupied Japan" mark is impressed on the bottom, accompanied by an outline of Mount Fuji. It is likely that vases of comparable quality exist, and collectors would be wise to inspect the mark of any piece of pottery or porcelain that they suspect might have been made during the Occupation.

Porcelain vases that might have been made during the Nippon period can also be found with the "Occupied" mark. Most of these are of good quality, but are overdecorated and usually gilded. The vases are decorative by themselves and do not adapt well to flower arranging.

291. Unusually handsome cylinder vase of buff pottery with coral bands. Height, 10 inches.

292. Mark incised on the bottom of the vase in Ill. 291.

293. Vase marked "Made in Occupied Japan" is of prewar quality and was probably a Noritake product. Hand-painted scene is Egyptian.

294. Miniature vases in porcelain. The tallest ones in the center are 3 inches.

By far the great majority of vases, both large and small, that can be found from the postwar era are poorly decorated versions of earlier Japanese export pieces. Many thousands of these were made. Most are of the miniature variety and measure less than three inches in height. Often sold by the pair, these are colorful imitations of Satsuma or Chinese export pieces. They were decorated with a combination of decal designs and thick slip outlines that appear to have been applied with a toothpaste tube. Heads and full figures of Orientals are the most prevalent decoration, but these small novelty items bear little resemblance to true Satsuma chinaware. Such porcelain novelties sold wholesale in 1950 for 65¢ a dozen—they were hardly made as works of art.

295. Group of miniature porcelain pitchers. The tallest is 2½ inches.

296. Miniature porcelain vases, two decorated with dragons. Height, 2½ inches.

297. Two Satsuma-style miniature vases and vase decorated with chrysanthemums in Chinese style.

298. Group of three miniature vases.

299. Miniature Satsuma-style vases. The second vase from the left was sold as a souvenir in Canada. The decal label was applied there.

For the inexpensive miniature vases the Japanese copied their own better-quality export ware, but they did not stop at this style. They also made miniature replicas of vases in Chinese style with allover patterns of flower forms. Tiny ewers and vases were made as copies of European pottery and porcelain too. Poor imitations of Wedgwood jasperware, three-dimensional flower decoration, and floral-decorated white porcelain ewers and vases were produced. Gilding is prevalent on even the least expensive of the vases, since the Japanese knew from experience that it appealed to the American buyer. The variety of shapes made is enormous.

FAIRY TALE MINIATURES

BP-5A   **Doz. .35**
Porcelain Novelty Assortment. Sizes
up to 2". Regular 10 cent values.
Packed 2 dozen assorted.
Minimum shipment 6 dozen.

300. Advertisement from a 1950 wholesale catalog illustrates the low price charged for miniature porcelain vases.

301. Pair of miniature vases in imitation Wedgwood with pink raised roses as decoration.

302. Pair of doves decorate a flowerpot.

303. Pottery duck painted in realistic colors is a planter.

Decorative containers for house plants were made in profusion; a popular one was the Mexican burro pulling a cart. Inevitably planted with ivy or philodendron, these sat on many American windowsills in the 1950s. Another popular style of planter was the rickshaw pulled by an Oriental peasant figure. An amusing variation of this style is the rickshaw puller at rest, playing his mandolin. Many of these planters were sold to florists, who had had a difficult time during the war finding inexpensive decorative containers.

As with most other porcelain and pottery made during the period of Occupation,

304. Caricature duck with top hat and bow tie.

305. Group of planters, all with the same theme.

306. Wheelbarrow planters. Piece on the right is a covered box, probably for cigarettes.

307. Rickshaw planters.

308. Rickshaw planters *(center and right)*. Planter at left is a man pushing a load of logs.

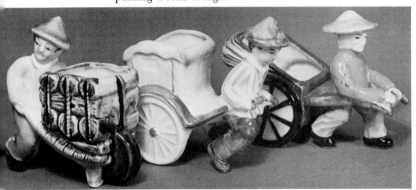

309. Unusual rickshaw planter with the man resting and playing the lute.

the Japanese were not shy about copying any pottery or porcelain technique used elsewhere in the world if they could do so well enough and inexpensively enough to compete on the American market. There are Delft-style pots and planters, Italian majolica flowerpots, Mexican-style vases, and copies of eighteenth-century German, French, and English porcelain vases. These would easily outsell pottery and porcelain vases and planters made elsewhere in the world, and their production at very low prices gave the wholesalers an enormous variety of inexpensive gift items to offer. Mostly, the miniature vases were of the dime-store type; the better-quality gift shops and department stores searched for and were supplied with larger vases and pots in great variety and of better quality.

It is the small, poorly decorated pieces of porcelain that gave the Japanese a reputation in the West for producing cheap and shoddy merchandise. Keep in mind, however, that the Japanese have, for centuries, produced excellent-quality pottery and porcelain. During the period of the Occupation, Japanese pottery and porcelain

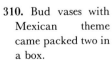

310. Bud vases with Mexican theme came packed two in a box.

311. Porcelain flower bowl with bright orange border and flowers and foliage decorated with enameled raised dots.

312. Unusual miniature vases. Center vase is an imitation of Italian majolica. Vase at right has sgraffito design.

makers simply gave the American customer what he wanted—decorative novelty items at very low prices. At the time it was merely a matter of finding products that would not compete with Western products; few of the pottery or porcelain vases or planters sent to America during the Occupation represented the Japanese facility for making fine porcelain or pottery. In Japan, the fictile arts have long been considered as important as fine painting or other art forms. Certainly, the bulk of the decorative vases and planters sent to America during the Occupation were considered only as products that would bring some necessary income to a country struggling to get back into sound economic order.

It is for their historical value rather than their artistic merit that Americans today search for the tiny overdecorated vases or the larger planters marked "Made in Occupied Japan." Perhaps one marked vase or planter out of two thousand will be of a quality comparable to the flower containers that are used by the Japanese themselves in the practice of their art of flower arranging. But the collecting of miniature "Occupied" vases, especially, has grown in the past few years as more and more collectors search only for miniature versions of larger art forms. This was a technique that the Japanese understood very well. The tiny vases and ewers in an almost endless variety of shapes and decoration that sold originally for no more than a quarter apiece are now in somewhat short supply, especially if they are marked "Made in Occupied Japan."

12

Lacquerware

Although the art of lacquerwork originated in China, there is documentation that the Japanese adapted this form of the decorative arts as early as the eighth century. The development of the lacquer process by the Japanese reached an artistic summit in the seventeenth century, when it was first introduced to the Europeans. English, French, and Dutch artisans attempted to learn the secret of producing lacquer that would approximate Oriental lacquer throughout the next two centuries, but they were never completely successful. Japanese lacquer remained in high demand and was an important export item.

As an item to be shipped abroad, Japanese lacquer had certain advantages. It was impervious to dampness and weather conditions that might affect other materials during shipping. It was virtually unbreakable when packed properly, and also light in weight. It is not surprising, therefore, to find that Japanese lacquer was one product American importers assumed would once again be popular with their countrymen when postwar trade resumed with the Japanese.

313. Coaster set: six coasters and a container. Each coaster has a different decoration. The set came in black, red, or green lacquer.

Unfortunately, prior to World War II, the Japanese had been making for export a cheap substitute for good-quality lacquer, and postwar importers found the American market less enthusiastic when quantities of Japanese lacquer appeared following the war. Since the prewar lacquerware had been only an inexpensive substitute for better lacquer, the art had deteriorated to a mass-market product that had sold for pennies. The lacquer coating on these items was thin and peeled easily. Few items with the durability and artistry of the older and finer lacquer were exported during the period between the two world wars. In fact, lacquer as a fine art was not understood by many twentieth-century Americans.

In comparison to decorative products in porcelain, very little lacquer was made for export during the Occupation of Japan. The few importers who understood the lacquer process, and hoped that the American market would accept a better-quality product than they had been used to, found themselves with warehouses full of handsome boxes, vases, bowls, cups, and plates for which there were few buyers. The "Made in Occupied Japan" mark did not help sell the product either, and it was not until collectors began to search for all products made by the Japanese during the Occupation that caches of lacquerware, still in its original packing, were finally sold.

Thus, oddly, it was no help to the importers that the lacquer made during the Occupation was generally of a better quality than the earlier shoddy product that had given Oriental lacquer a bad name. Also, the production of lacquer of the type

314. Set of six plates, black lacquer, 6¾ inches in diameter.

315. Individual serving bowls, black lacquer with a different floral painting on each piece. Diameter, 4¾ inches.

imported after the war required a lot of handwork and the shapes and decoration used were modern in appearance rather than traditional. The retail prices were high in comparison to the prices for prewar lacquer. Another problem was that American customers did not trust the claims of the importers that lacquer was not injured "by alcohol, edible salts or food acids." The few importers, mostly ex-GI's who risked their capital on the lacquer market, had a difficult time selling it to a skeptical American market, and most of them went broke. In lacquer, as well as with some other products, the Japanese artisans, by manufacturing shoddy merchandise before the war, had ruined their own reputations.

There is a great deal of difference between older lacquer products from Japan and those made for export during the first half of this century. Japanese lacquer is a natural product derived from the sap of a sumac tree *(Rhus vernicifera)* that grows wild in China but is cultivated in Japan. This sap contains urushi acid, the property that makes Oriental lacquer impervious to water marks and other staining. It is the way in which this raw material was refined, processed, and utilized that remained a secret from the European artisans who tried vainly to copy Japanese lacquer.

In the early days, most Japanese lacquer items were made of a core of white pinewood *(Retinispora obtusa)*, which is fine grained and free from knots and resins. The

316. Covered soup bowls were made in black or red lacquer. Size: 4¾ by 2¼ inches. A set consisted of six bowls with covers.

317. Fruit bowl *(foreground)* is black and buff with red branches and buff flowers. Ten inches in diameter. Plate in rear was used as serving dish or cabinet piece.

wood was planed to a degree of thinness seldom found in any Western woodwork. It is this preparation of the wood core of lacquer items that differentiates the good early lacquer from most lacquer products made for export in this century. The core of the later lacquer is of heavier wood, and the lacquer applications—often more than fifty coats in the older work—were cut to a minimum. In the earlier work, a core could also be made of paper, cloth, or metal; after numerous applications of lacquer, the product was mostly made of lacquer. The postwar lacquer products were made almost entirely of wood with only a thin coating of lacquer.

In the early days, an artist sometimes devoted years to the making and decorating of a single lacquer item, but by the nineteenth century the industry became large enough—particularly when Japan began large-scale trade with the West after 1859—to necessitate newer and faster methods of manufacture in order to satisfy foreign

318. Serving tray, black lacquer, with gold decoration. Size: 8 inches by 12 inches.

markets. Although the inferior product still required a substantial amount of hand-work, the exported postwar lacquer cannot be considered an art form.

Since the only lacquer to be considered here is that produced during the Occupa-tion, it is important that the process used during this period be described and com-pared with earlier processes for producing lacquerware. Thus, it will be easier to understand the differences and the similarities of the two types of products. Even with the shortcuts used to make the later lacquerware, it will be easy to understand why this particular product is still among the most artistic of the many decorative products introduced to Americans following the war.

First, the process for making the older type of lacquer helps us understand why this lengthy and painstaking work could no longer be done. In making any type of lacquer, the sap must first be drawn from the sumac tree. This was done by making an incision in the bark and scraping the inside of the trunk with a spatula-like tool. Once the lac was extracted, it was pressed through layers of cotton cloth to remove any impurities, such as pieces of bark or dirt. Exposure to air turns the raw lacquer from white to brown and then to black.

In the old days, the lacquer was ground to a homogeneous liquid in a wooden tub. The liquid was again strained, and the moisture was evaporated from it by exposure to the sun or to artificial heat. During this process, workmen stirred the liquid constantly. Coloring agents were then added, depending on the type of lacquer required. The colors most often used for the older lacquer were aventurine (copper brown), cinnabar (orange red), black, and chestnut. Two very rare colors were green and white.

After the joiner had painstakingly made a core for a lacquer object of the white pinewood (or one of the other materials already mentioned), and had filled all joints and crevices and carefully sanded the piece to the desired thinness and smoothness, the second step in lacquering would take place. The object was prepared to take the coats of lacquer by the application of a mixture of rice paste and lacquer mixed with cotton wadding. This was pasted over all the joints and nail holes to ensure further strength and smoothness. When this mixture had dried, all surfaces of the object were spread with a thin coat of lacquer sizing to fill up the pores of the wood. Then followed another application of paste that contained ground pottery as well as the rice paste and lac mixture. When this second coat had dried, the piece was then polished with a fine sandstone.

319. Three-piece salad bowl set in black lacquer. Bowl is 10 inches in diameter.

320. Nut bowl serving set (eight pieces) is gold on the inside and black lacquer on the outside. Each piece is decorated by hand with a different design. Bowl, 5¾ by 2 inches. Dishes, 1½ by 1 inch.

The object was next covered with a layer of Japanese rice paper or thin hemp cloth, the layer being affixed with a mixture of rice paste and more lac. This was done to prevent warping and to give the object tensile strength. Several more coats of lacquer and paste mixture were then applied, dried, and rubbed by hand.

The drying process for lacquer must be done in a damp atmosphere, to prevent the lacquer from running or drying unevenly. A final preparatory coat of lacquer containing pulverized ocher and ground pottery was then applied, and India ink was often rubbed into the surface before the very last coat of lacquer was applied. A lengthy drying process between all coats was necessary, and finally the object would be carefully rubbed with a special kind of fine-grained charcoal. The piece was at last ready for decoration.

Many forms of decoration were used on the earlier lacquerware, but most of these painstaking designs required the work of special skilled artists and so had been abandoned for more simple designs for the lacquer made for export well before World War II. In the nineteenth century, however, many heavily decorated objects were made almost exclusively for export, the Japanese preferring plain or simple painted decorations. Few of the earlier decorating methods were carried over to the "Occupied Japan" lacquer pieces.

321. Nut set in all-black lacquer; measurements are the same as for the set shown in Ill. 320.

One of the earliest forms of decoration was sprinkling gold powder over a russet brown lacquer ground. Gold foil was used from the beginning of the eighteenth century for lacquer decoration. The foil was arranged by hand in minute squares on the surface of an object, which was then again lacquered and polished.

The finest early export lacquer pieces were those that were artist decorated with hand paintings of an almost limitless variety of motifs. Landscapes, seascapes, birds, fish, insects, flowers, and animals were used, as well as formal arrangements of scrolls, arabesques, and diaper patterns. Gold was usually the predominant color, but green, red, blue, and silver were used as well. On the most important pieces, all surfaces were decorated—it was not unusual for the inside surfaces of boxes and the undersides of lids to be as carefully decorated as the exteriors.

Relief designs were applied to some pieces by the use of a putty foundation, which was applied, dried, and then hand modeled. A few boxes with this type of high-relief decoration have been found marked "Made in Occupied Japan," but these are scarce enough to assume that pieces decorated by this method might have been made before the war and marked later, so that they could be exported. Inlays of metal such as gold, silver, and pewter, as well as of mother-of-pearl, were also used on some prewar lacquer objects, and these may turn up with the "Occupied Japan" mark.

By 1900 the Japanese lacquer industry was producing articles in great quantity for export to Europe and America. Many of these were quite elaborate and designed for only Western taste. The quality of the lacquerwork declined as the demand for Japanese artwork became stronger, and although it was possible to mechanize the industry to some degree, a lot of handwork was still necessary in the manufacture of the product. Eventually, a kind of lacquerware was developed that resembled the original product but did not have the properties of the old lacquer. It was made mostly of wood, and the coats of lacquer were cut to a minimum. Within a short time, this lacquer would peel, and the painted decorations were clearly the work of assembly-line artists.

Following World War II at least one American importer (Crockery Importers of Newington, Connecticut) attempted to revive an interest in quality lacquerware made in Japan in styles suited to the American taste. Many of the items imported were handsome and useful, but American customers were skeptical about claims that the

322. Pieces of "Made in Occupied Japan" lacquer cut away so that the wooden core and the lacquer thickness can be seen. This was done so that salesmen could demonstrate the quality and strength of the product.

tumblers would stand up to repeated use or that the soup dishes or teacups would last at all if used more than a few times. Japanese-style products, especially those that would have to be expensive for the time at the retail level, were not in favor with Americans after the war; it soon became obvious that the products that sold best were those that were imitations of European products. Few Americans understood that quality lacquer was almost a lost art, and it seemed that no amount of salesmanship on the part of the importer would empty his warehouse of the postwar lacquerware in which he had invested rather heavily. In an attempt to help his customers better understand his product, the importer even wrote a description of how the lacquer was produced. For today's collector of products marked "Made in Occupied Japan," this record is invaluable. It explains the willingness of the Japanese to return to ancient methods of production in order to produce products to sell abroad.

For the postwar lacquer, at least twenty-five steps were involved, consuming about six man-hours of labor for an average small item. The importer complained that the bulk of the raw lacquer used during that period had to be imported from China and had tripled in price within a few years following the war, and that there was "no prospect of improvement." Various types of wood were used for the core material. Cherry, birch, chestnut, and cypress, all woods native to Japan, were utilized. Chestnut was used for bowls and cherry wood for wine cups. The lumber used was green and had to be kiln-dried by burning sawdust in crude ovens. The machinery for turning was also crude and simple, and was mounted on the floor rather than on benches, since "the artisans preferred working on the floor."

The oldtime (prewar) lacquer factories no longer existed; the bulk of the "Occupied Japan" lacquerware was made by home industries where every member of a family helped. Each family specialized in a single phase of the industry, which was divided roughly into three segments: turning, preparing the lacquerware for the design, and painting the final decoration.

As already explained, the major difference between oldtime lacquerware and the lacquer imported after the war was that the later product was made mostly of turned wood. Pure, clear lacquer was used as glue when two pieces of wood were joined.

323. Seven-piece shot cup set is black lacquer with gold on the inside of the cups. Tray, 7 inches in diameter.

324. Powder box, gold lacquer, came in a set of two: one for the dresser, 4 inches by 2 inches, and this purse size, 4 inches by 1 inch.

Teacup handles, the bases of fruit bowls, and sometimes the larger trays were joined in this manner. Often the trays were laminated with several different pieces of wood, to give them strength and to prevent future warping. As for the older lacquer, moisture was needed while the lac was drying, and so during the drying process the work was stored in wooden cabinets the walls of which were wetted down to provide the necessary dampness. The importer claimed that once lacquer was dry, "*nothing* would dissolve it."

Because of the situation that prevailed during the Occupation, the industrial organization was very loose and industries were congregated in various "centers," each having a distinctive design, style of decoration, and type of workmanship. Every center had an association that helped its members in obtaining raw material and in sales problems. The members of the centers tried to avoid competition with one another by specializing in a single item such a wine cups, trays, or bowls. The "houses" were all independent of one another, but were loosely connected by a "master," who obtained orders, raw materials, and financing. The "master" was also responsible for seeing that orders from abroad were expedited.

Following the processes used for making the lacquer that was placed on the American market after the war makes it apparent that for a short while the ancient art of making quality lacquer for export had a revival in Japan. Although the process

325. Demitasse cups, black with gold interiors. Size of cups, 2⅝ inches by 1⅝ inches.

326. Teacup set, black with gold interiors. Size: cups, 3⅜ inches by 1⅞ inches.

was used for objects that were modern in application and appearance, and certain shortcuts were taken, collectors who are aware of this revival of a Japanese art form should have a great deal of respect for "Occupied Japan" lacquerware. It is one of the few quality handmade products to come from that short period in Japanese-American history.

Turning (making the wooden shape of the object to be lacquered) required a half hour for the first rough shaping of the green lumber. Kiln-drying took three days; then another half hour was needed for the finished turning of the dried wood. Following this, the first coat of lacquer was applied, and this coat, in which the lac was mixed with pulverized burnt clay, took twenty-four hours to dry. Afterward, the article was rubbed down with a piece of charcoal. This process was repeated at least three times, but for the more expensive ware a piece might be given as many as seven coats, with twenty-four hours of drying time required between each coat. Next an inferior lacquer was used as a base coat; the piece was dried again, and a body coat of refined lacquer in red, green, or black was applied and dried. The piece was then ready for decoration.

Each color in the decoration had to be painted separately, and have a minimum drying time of five hours to prevent the colors from running together. The number of steps and the time involved in finishing the decoration depended on how elaborate the design was to be and the eventual value of the finished product. The importer claimed that an average of seven steps was required for commercial products. Although this did not equal the number of steps (often as many as one hundred) used in making art lacquerware for domestic use, it is unlikely that that superb type of lacquer was produced in any amount during the period of the Occupation.

327. Wine cups decorated with a long-tailed cock and a plum branch. The tray was not part of the original set, which consisted of six cups only. Height of cups: 4¾ inches.

328. Tumblers, gold interiors, black on the outside with a variety of bird decoration.

The minimum delivery time required to make a piece of the export lacquer during the Occupation might have been about ten days, if a crew worked two shifts. But the importer also complained that shift work did not exist in Japan, and so the best that production time could have been was about twenty days. Shift work was not practical, since the workmen would be sitting around waiting for the lacquer to dry; also, most of them worked at other jobs too. Therefore, the normal time needed to complete an order was from two to three months.

There were other problems involved in the manufacture of lacquerware products. Lacquer does not reach its true color until it has dried. At the time of painting, the red color is a deep brown and the black is not the jet black to be found on the finished product. After the application of each color and the five-hour drying process, the brush is cleaned with mineral or vegetable oil, and then washed out with gasoline. Lacquer will not harden if there is any oil in it.

Since many of the "Occupied Japan" pieces of lacquer are finished in gold, it is important that the process for this type of decoration also be understood. Although gold decoration has never been especially popular in Japan itself, Japanese artisans have long understood the Westerner's fondness for this color and have used heavy gold decoration on many of the art products made for export. The process for gilding lacquerware includes the dusting of twenty-four-karat gold powder on a sticky surface. Although the surface of a gold piece appears to have been painted on, this is not the case. Instead, clear lacquer was rubbed on the surface with a wad of cloth; only the slightest amount of lacquer was needed. Using a leather wad, the artist then picked up the gold powder and lightly tamped the surface until the entire object was coated. The gold powder supply on the wad was replenished as needed. The surface was rubbed with the same wad to spread the gold powder evenly over the object. The piece was given its five-hour drying, and the process repeated at least three or four times until the desired thickness of gold lacquer was obtained. With each coat, the piece took on a deeper and richer color. After this, the piece was decorated with colors, each requiring a five-hour drying period between applications.

The final step necessary in making the "Occupied Japan" lacquerware was to apply a trademark and the necessary import identification of either "Occupied Japan" or "Made in Occupied Japan." This was done by smearing a thin coat of lacquer on a flat surface with the appropriate rubber stamp and dusting it over with the gold.

Obviously, the method of making lacquerware in Japan in the post-World War II period was shortened somewhat in comparison to that used in earlier times. Because of the expense of lacquer, the cost of the lengthy handwork, and the time involved in the manufacture, the process had to be modified to a great degree. Most "Occupied Japan" lacquerware is of a quality that surpasses that of the lacquer made for export prior to the war, although it still does not compare to eighteenth- and nineteenth-century lacquer. In the "Occupied Japan" products, the greater part of the object is wood rather than layers of lacquer. However, the shapes made were mostly practical rather than merely decorative, new designs and shapes geared to the American market being devised. Teacups, shot cup sets, demitasse sets, serving trays, wine cups, cordial sets, coasters, salad bowls, fruit bowls, and tea sets were among the more practical items. Decorative boxes, jewel boxes, and vases were also made. Although the prices charged seem low to us today, they were high enough to discourage Americans from purchasing the products when they were new. Since the ware was not commercially successful, relatively little of it exists for today's collectors.

Although few of the lacquerware products made during the Occupation have been used to any extent, time has proved that the quality was exceptionally good. No warping seems to have taken place, and even the small boxes lined with silk have not crazed or peeled; in fact, no warping is evident in any of the products. It is impossible to detect seams in the wood bases of any of the products. The hand paintings on the pieces of postwar lacquerware are often not of a quality that can be considered fine art, but they are colorful and they do fit the style of the pieces.

Although the short revival of lacquerware that occurred during the period of the Occupation may not have been commercially successful, it was artistically successful if

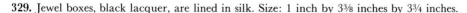

329. Jewel boxes, black lacquer, are lined in silk. Size: 1 inch by 3⅜ inches by 3¾ inches.

one compares the lacquer to many of the other products that were made. The demand among collectors of "Made in Occupied Japan" objects for the good-quality lacquerware is high, and it is unfortunate that the supply is so limited. It was the American customer's resistance to decorative objects that "looked" Japanese, along with the lack of understanding of how lacquer was made and decorated, and skepticism about its durability, that caused the manufacturers of the product to abandon it. Obviously, today's hourly wages in Japan would preclude the resumption of the manufacture of good-quality lacquer for export in any quantity.

LACQUERWARE

WHOLESALE PRICE LIST F.O.B. NEWINGTON, CONN.
·Terms: 2% 10 days net 30

15, May. 1951

330. Original price list (wholesale) for lacquerware imported in 1951. Lacquer of this quality was expensive when new, and is worth many times its original price today.

No.	DESCRIPTION	Price $
2-11	**WINE CUPS**—6 pc. Cock & Plum branch.	4.20
2-13	**WINE CUPS & TRAY**—7 pc. set-Gold finish	10.95
2-15	**CORDIAL CUPS & TRAY**—7 pc. set-Gold finish	5.75
2-16	**SHOT CUPS & TRAY**—7 pc. set	5.25
3-11	**TEA CUPS & SAUCERS**—Red or Black-per ½ doz.	10.00
3-12	**DEMI TASSE**—short-Per ½ dozen	8.25
3-13	**DEMI TASSE**—Tall-Per ½ dozen	8.25
4-11	**TRAY**—Buff & Black	5.00
4-12	**TRAY**—Plant design	5.00
4-14	**TRAY**—Cock & Plum branch design	3.50
5-11	**PLATE**—Pink & Black Flower	2.25
5-12	**PLATE**—Leaf design inlaid in gold	2.50
5-13	**PLATE**— Assorted designs-per ½ dozen	9.50
6-11	**FRUIT BOWL**—Black & buff	4.75
7-11	**BOWL**—Red with gold inlaid design	1.50
7-12	**BOWL**—Assorted designs-per ½ dozen	6.50
7-13	**SALAD BOWL SET**— 3 pc.	6.00
7-16	**SOUP BOWL WITH COVER**—per ½ dozen	9.00
8-11	**JEWEL BOX**—Black with gold flower	4.00
8-12	**COASTERS**—6 dishes & container-Red-Black-Green	3.25
8-13	**COASTERS**—6 dishes & container-Gold	4.50
8-14	**JEWEL BOX**	.75
9-11	**POWDER CONTAINERS**—Set of 2-Gold	4.25
10-11	**NUT BOWL SERVING SET**—8 pc. inside gold	4.50
12-11	**VASE**—each	6.25

NOT ILLUSTRATED

2-10	**SHERBET CUPS**—Red-Black-6 pc. set	9.00
2-17	**WHISKEY SET**—Black-Decanter, Tray, 6 shot cups	12.50
3-14	**TEA SERVING SET**—Black-Tray, Creamer, Sugar, Tea pot	14.50
3-15	**TEA SERVING SET**—Gold-Tray, Creamer, Sugar, Tea pot	19.00
4-15	**TRAY**—For demi-tasse cups	6.00
7-14	**SALAD BOWL SET**—4 pc.	9.50
7-15	**SALAD BOWL SET**—with 6 plates	10.00
8-18	**COASTERS**—8 dishes & container-Red-Black-Green	3.75
8-19	**COASTERS**—8 dishes & container-Gold	4.75
13-11	**NAPKIN RINGS**—Black-Red-6 pc. set	2.00
13-12	**NAPKIN RINGS**—Gold-6 pc. set	3.00
15-11	**SALAD FORK & SPOON**—Black	2.50

13

Metal

Many small metal objects were made for export during the Occupation. Few were of good quality, and the more than quarter century that has passed since the metal gift and souvenir pieces were produced has been somewhat unkind to most of them. When anything in metal marked "Made in Occupied Japan" turns up today in pristine condition, it can be considered a "find" for the collector. It must be remembered that most of the metal objects were made to sell for a few cents at tourist places—they were not meant to be museum pieces or collector's items.

The majority of the metal souvenir pieces were small ashtrays and pin trays. Most often these were stamped from the white metal called antimony, an element of metallic appearance and crystalline structure. It is tin white in color and is hard and brittle. Although it is not likely that any of the white metal used by Japanese manufacturers in making objects for export is pure antimony, that element was added to other metals to produce small stamped ashtrays and other objects during the Occupation. In comparison to the number of pieces made in porcelain and other ceramics,

331. Ashtray, souvenir of San Francisco.

certainly fewer pieces were made of metal and a comparatively small number of these have survived. Plated metal was an especially poor choice for ashtrays or any other objects that required washing. The trays were given a coating of shiny material that peeled easily, and so they became rather unattractive with a few years' use. These pieces had the appearance of having been silver plated, but it is difficult to say today

332. Ashtray, souvenir of New York City.

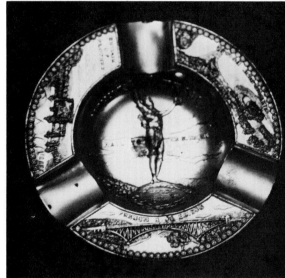

333. Ashtray, souvenir of the Mohawk Trail.

334. Pin tray, souvenir of New York.

335. Pin tray, souvenir of Fort Ticonderoga.

exactly what method was used to give them an attractive surface when they were new.

Since the metal souvenir items are somewhat scarce today, even collectors who prefer to purchase only items in good condition are not reluctant to buy peeling ashtrays or blackened boxes as long as they are marked "Made in Occupied Japan." There are, of course, some white metal objects that were never used, and these have remained in excellent condition. Still other metal objects seem to have been made of better-quality material or were made only for display, and so still look fairly new.

Most of the souvenir items are more valuable today for the places in the United States that they represent and for their historical value than they are for their intrinsic beauty. "Occupied Japan" souvenirs have been found that were sold in Niagara Falls, Washington, D.C., New York City, and at many other tourist attractions that became popular again as soon as gas rationing was removed and Americans were able to travel freely for the first time since the war. One especially desirable item of this type is a silver-colored ashtray with a view of the proposed United Nations buildings. The tray has brightly enameled flags of the United Nations in its border.

Salt and pepper shakers of white metal were also made for American souvenir seekers. Among the most desirable for today's collectors are small figures of the Statue of Liberty and the Empire State Building. These were part of a three-piece set that included a tray. Many other shaker sets were made in metal too, including at least one chrome-plated set with plastic handles. The shakers are in the shape of miniature coffeepots, and both they and the tray have plastic handles. The design is typical of the Art Deco style of the thirties, and this set was probably made before the war as well as after. Also of better-quality metal is a tea-leaf holder in the form of a minia-

336. Ashtray, souvenir of Niagara Falls.　337. Crumb tray, souvenir of Washington, D.C.

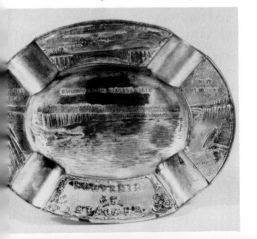

338. Pin tray depicting the proposed United Nations buildings. Note the enameled flags on the border.

339. Salt and pepper shakers, souvenirs of Penn's Cave.

340. Salt and pepper shakers on a tray, souvenirs of New York.

341. Shaker set in the shape of coffeepots has red plastic handles and is in the style of the 1930s.

342. Tea strainer is a souvenir of Grand Canyon National Park. Salt and pepper shakers of white metal have a shiny finish that peeled off easily.

ture teapot. The perforated pot sits on its own small saucer; a tag on a link chain shows the piece to have been a souvenir of Grand Canyon National Park in Arizona.

Many boxes for jewelry or cigarettes were made of white metal. These have stood up fairly well. The jewelry boxes are lined with fine silk under which soft cotton is glued. Only when the boxes were enameled, as many of the small piano-shaped pieces were, is the condition poor. The enamel paint peeled so easily that many of these boxes have scars to show where the original price tag was pasted. When the tag was removed, so was a patch of enamel.

Besides the piano boxes, boxes were made in many other shapes and designs. There are some cigarette and jewel boxes in white metal with embossed Oriental motifs and others decorated with Western-style motifs and designs.

There were many smoking sets made of metal. These usually consist of a tray, a lighter, and some sort of holder for cigarettes. Collectors search for lighters made in the shape of cowboy boots, or hats, pistols, or pens, since these are the rarities. Many other lighters were copies of lighters that had been made in the United States in silver

343. Piano jewel box lined with silk. The top is enameled in red. *Author's Collection*

344. Lyre-shaped and piano-shaped jewel boxes with their lids enameled in blue.

345. Piano cigarette box with a removable ashtray under which is a music box mechanism. Length, 6 inches.

346. Jewel box and cigarette box with Japanese decoration on the covers.

347. Stamp box *(left)* and cigarette box; white metal.

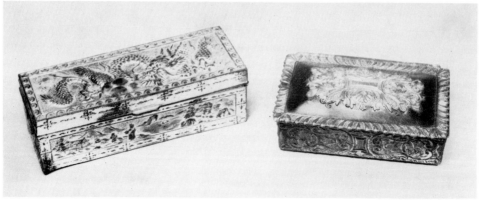

or silver plate before the war. One of the most interesting and unusual lighters is the "Camera Table Lighter" called the "Cont-Lite." This lighter looks like a miniature camera on a tripod. The "camera" has a green plastic lens and viewfinder; the front of the case is embossed with flowers and the back has a dragon design. The tripod unscrews so that the lighter can also be carried in one's pocket. Both the tripod and the lighter are embossed with the mark "Made in Occupied Japan."

One of the most unusual and impractical smoking accessories to be found is a white metal ashtray with an embossed and colorfully enameled border of flowers and dragons. The center of the tray has a clear glass dome under which is encased a

348 A, B, & C. Figural cigarette lighters in white metal. The cowboy boot is a cigarette holder, but the shape was also made as a lighter. The chrome auto lighter is a rarity. **A & B.** *Joseph P. Valenti;* **C.** *Author's Collection*

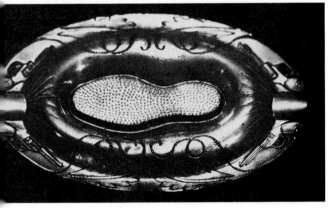

349. Ashtray with boot-shape depression was part of a smoking set. A cowboy boot lighter fit into the depression.

350. Smoking set in white metal with gadroon borders.

351. Lighter and ashtray set in plated white metal.

monarch butterfly. Since the piece has cigarette-rest depressions in the border, it is obvious that the original stamping was for an ashtray, but it would be impossible to lay a cigarette in it without scorching the butterfly under the glass. For this reason, if this tray can be found today, it is usually in "like new" condition.

Perhaps the most successful metal objects made were the animal figures, mostly horses. These appear to have been made of a white metal finished in a bronze-color coating. Today's collector should be aware that copies of the horse shown in Illustration 358 are now on the market marked "U.S.A." Be certain that the "Made in Occupied Japan" mark is clear before buying horses that seem to have been made from the same mold.

Metal incense burners in the shape of pagodas and Shinto temples can be found. These items were popular as souvenirs and were purchased in some quantity by the GI's stationed in Japan during the Occupation. They were also exported and sold as souvenir items in this country.

352 A. Camera table lighter and its original box. The lighter unscrews from the tripod, to be used as pocket lighter. Both parts are marked "Made in Occupied Japan." **B.** Same lighter was made with a black molded plastic case rather than one of chased metal. **A.** *Joseph P. Valenti;* **B.** *Author's Collection*

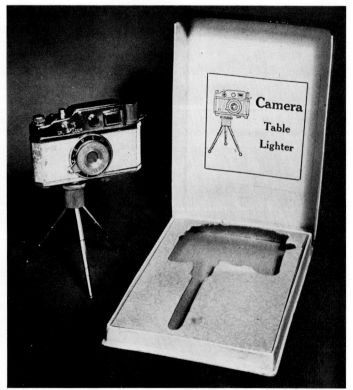

353. White metal ashtray with a monarch butterfly encased in a glass dome in the center.

354. Cornucopia-shape plated white metal cigarette lighter. *Author's Collection*

355. Horseshoe-shaped ashtray with the figure of a horse.

356. White metal ashtray decorated with a swan figure.

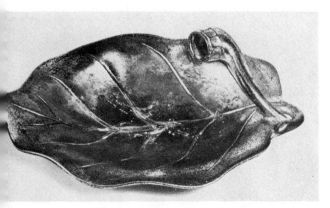

357. Ashtray in the shape of a tobacco leaf has a pipe as decoration. Copper with silver-colored plating. *Author's Collection*

358. Horse figure in bronzed metal. Length, 6 inches.

Perhaps the least successful—artistically or practically—of all white metal objects made for export were the candleholders made in shapes copied from American or European candlesticks or candelabra. When cleaned of wax after being used a few times, the shiny plating came off, and these candlesticks usually are found today in rather sorry condition.

359. Incense burner, copper, is a Japanese teahouse with a thatched roof.

360. Double candleholder in white metal.

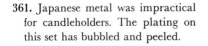

361. Japanese metal was impractical for candleholders. The plating on this set has bubbled and peeled.

The metal objects that seem to have withstood time and use somewhat better than the antimony pieces are those made of copper with silver plating. These pieces are heavier, less prone to breakage, and when the plating wears off, the copper body is not objectionable. Also, on these pieces the plating wears off rather than peels.

Other copper-base products that were successful and are often found in very good condition are those of lacquered copper. Lacquer is a product that the Japanese understood and used to its best advantage. Since the lacquered metal giftware made during the Occupation was a better-quality product to begin with, and was made to be sold in gift shops rather than in souvenir shops and roadside stands, more effort was put into its design and manufacture. Red and black lacquered metal trays and baskets can be found today that are handsomely decorated and still in pristine condition. Although made in less quantity than the cheaper metal pieces, lacquered metal tobacco jars, candy dishes, and a few other shapes can still be found.

362. Pierced white metal bonbon dish.

363. Advertisement from a 1950 wholesale catalog for miniature copper kettles with solid brass trim.

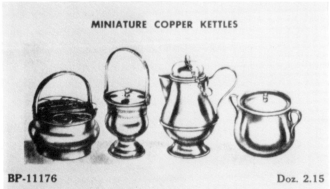

MINIATURE COPPER KETTLES

BP-11176   Doz. 2.15

Novelty Copper Kettle Assortment. Solid copper with solid brass trim. 5 Styles. Sizes up to 3½". Sturdily constructed.

Packed 1 dozen assorted to box.

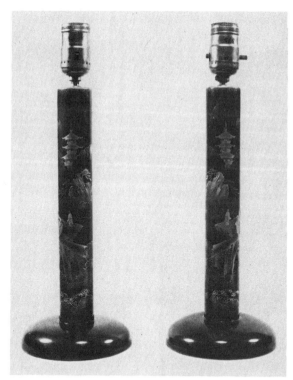

364 A. Lacquer-over-copper basket has gold decal decoration on black. B. Handsome pair of lamp bases (height, 12 inches) are hand decorated in raised silver, pewter, and a gold scenic design with pearl-shell inlay on red lacquered metal. This type of lacquer with the "Made in Occupied Japan" mark is very rare. A. *Joseph P. Valenti;* B. *Mr. and Mrs. Frank Forshaw*

365. Lacquer-on-metal relish tray—red lacquer with gold decoration.

Even before the invention of the transistor and the age of miniaturization, the Japanese had been manufacturing miniature cameras and other objects of metal that had a practical use. The cameras, especially, were popular items with resident American soldiers in Japan during the Occupation, and some of these were exported for sale in the United States. Most of them are now obsolete and the film used in them is no longer being made. However, the cameras are prime collector's items with people who specialize in the history of photography. Some are quite tiny, no larger than a couple of inches. Two are illustrated here. The "Petal" model, in its original wooden case, is 1¾ inches in diameter. Included in the case for this round camera is a box holding a metal template, which can be used as a pattern from which a round piece of film is cut. Film is still available for this camera, but it has to be cut to order every time a picture is to be taken. This camera is now a prime collector's item. The "Tone"

366. "Petal," a round miniature camera in its original packing box. Camera measures less than 2 inches. Included in the package is a metal template for cutting round film.

367. "Tone," a miniature camera, is 3 inches long. Both case and camera are marked "Made in Occupied Japan."

camera and leather case in Illustration 367 is 2½ inches wide; it used film that is no longer being made, although a knowledgeable photographer could possibly modify film for it. These are only two examples of the ingenuity of the Japanese in the field of photographic equipment. Present-day photographers are well aware that Japan is today a leading exporter of superb photographic equipment.

Binoculars and opera glasses were other products made during the Occupation and exported in some quantity. Since optical equipment of all kinds was a type of production that undoubtedly continued and was encouraged throughout the war, the Japanese had the manufacturing capability to produce these items for export once trade resumed after the war. Other wartime equipment that was adapted to household objects for export during the Occupation included sewing machines and typewriters. However, these products did not find a particularly good market in the United States. Few are still in use today, and as collector's items they are difficult to find. Other early exports in metal were garden tools and fishing equipment.

Obviously, the collector who limits his or her purchasing to figurines and other ceramic products is missing a challenge. There are many fascinating metal objects still to be discovered that are marked "Made in Occupied Japan." Musical instruments

368. Miniature harmonica (2½ inches) was one of many musical instruments made for export.

369. Binoculars marked "Made in Occupied Japan."

370. A sewing machine that runs on batteries was among the first products shipped to the United States during the Occupation. *Author's Collection*

from kazoos to harmonicas were made and exported during the Occupation. All products made by the Japanese during the Occupation should be of interest to the collector who wants to own examples representing all the types of production that helped the Japanese regain their position as leaders in world trade. Many of the metal objects made may not be beautiful, but they do represent a time in history when the Japanese illustrated a remarkable amount of ingenuity in their manufacturing.

14

Paper, Wood, and Cloth

During the Occupation, a great many objects produced in Japan were made of paper, cloth, and wood. Most of these were exceptionally inexpensive when they were new, and many were semidisposable. Few of the paper items, especially, have lasted, and since they are so scarce they are among the most desirable of collectibles marked "Made in Occupied Japan." Many others were marked only on their boxes or with paper labels, and these objects are unidentifiable today.

The Japanese had been exceptionally adept at making a variety of paper items for export throughout this century, and production of such items probably resumed soon after trade opened up after the war. Collapsible paper lanterns, parasols in many sizes, Christmas tree decorations, and various other items are still being produced. Paper and cloth fans have been a staple export, and papier-mâché giftware, which is often confused with lacquerware in this country, can still be found in American gift shops from time to time.

Although there were not a great many items made from wood, one novelty

372. Fake cigar "exploded" into fan-shaped stars and stripes when lighted.

371. Paper-cover needle book. The mark can be seen along the bottom under the picture. *Peter Tavera*

373. Woven raffia Japanese finger trap is a child's trick toy. When a finger is stuck in either end, no amount of pulling will release them. Release comes when the fingers are pushed toward each other. *Author's Collection*

374. Turned coasters with handsome wood grain.

375. Wood and metal serving tray has a circular stamp on the back that reads "Hand-Crafted in Occupied Japan."

376. Wooden blocks probably used to teach the English language to the Japanese during the Occupation. Letters are in red or black. The blocks are extremely rare.

cigarette box is in short supply and strong demand among O.J. collectors. The box is made of imitation wood-grain inlay. A long-billed bird is perched on a log at one side of it, and when a lever is turned, the bird whistles a few notes, leans over, and pulls a cigarette from a drawer that pops open. This box is marked with a paper label that may be missing on the few examples that can still be found.

Utilitarian wooden objects such as salad bowls, metal-trimmed trays, carpenters' rulers, and bamboo stocking driers were also exported. Artists' paintbrushes were produced too. Cup stands were made in a variety of styles, and one was often packed in a single box with a cup and saucer for display. These "sets" made a popular gift package that usually sold for less than a dollar.

A few hand-carved wooden figurines were made, and these are in very short

377. Musical cigarette box. When the drum is pushed down, the bird bends over and picks out a cigarette from the drawer that opens.

BRUSHES
ARTIST — MARKING — BRONZING — LACQUERING

ARTIST BRUSHES
(IMPORTED)

BP-10101

Artist Brushes. Fine quality camel hair. Natural pointed ends for school and professional use. Nickel plated ferrules, black lacquered handles.

Lot No.	Size	Doz.
BP-10101/1	1	.33
BP-10101/2	2	.34
BP-10101/3	3	.35
BP-10101/4	4	.38
BP-10101/5	5	.50
BP-10101/6	6	.60
BP-10101/7	7	.70

Made in Occupied Japan
Packed 2 dozen of a size to envelope.

BP-10725   **Doz. Cds. .70**

Camel Hair Artist Brushes. (Imported). Good quality. Sizes 2, 4, 6. 3 on card.

Made in Occupied Japan.

Packed 1 dozen cards to box.

BP-15153   **Doz. .75**

Camel Hair Marking Brushes. (Imported.) Natural camel hair, full pointed, nickel plated ferrule, 12" natural wood handle. Very fine quality. Can be used for sign painting. Asst. 6 brushes of each size 1 to 4.
Made in Occupied Japan.
Packed 2 dozen on card.

BP-11108   **Doz. .65**

Black Bristled Marking Brushes. (Imported). Tinned ferrules. 12" Natural wood handles. Sizes 1 to 4.
Made in Occupied Japan.
Packed 1 dozen on card.

BP-10106   **Doz. 1.00**

Goat Hair Lacquer Brushes. (Imported.) Real Goat hair. Natural shaped ends 1¼" full oval head. Nickel plated ferrules, heavy marbelized handle. Size 8½".
Made in Occupied Japan.
Packed 2 dozen on card.

PENCIL ERASER

BP-50238   **Doz. .15**

Erasers. (Imported). Fine quality. Real rubber. All red. Size 2".
Made in Occupied Japan.
Packed 12 dozen to box.

BP-50235/1   **Doz. .21**

Erasers. (Imported.) Same as BP-50238. Larger size, 2⅝".
Made in Occupied Japan.
Packed 3 dozen to box.

INK and PENCIL ERASER

BP-50235/2   **Doz. .23**

Erasers. (Imported.) Fine quality. Real rubber. Two color combination for Ink and Pencil. Size 2⅝".
Made in Occupied Japan.
Packed 3 dozen to box.

BP-50236   **Doz. .32**

Erasers. (Imported.) Same as BP-50235/2. Larger size, 3⅝".
Made in Occupied Japan.
Packed 1 dozen to box.

RUBBER BANDS

BP-12185   **Doz. Envelopes .36**

Rubber Bands. (Imported.) Real rubber. Assorted colors and sizes. ½ oz. Printed cellophane envelope.

Made in Occupied Japan

Packed 2 dozen envelopes to box.

---

378. Artists' brushes, erasers, and rubber bands were among thousands of products made in Japan for export in 1950.

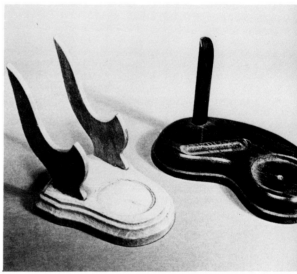

379. Wooden cup stands were sold separately or included in the box with a cup and saucer. Many types were made.

380. Folding rule, of wood and steel, as shown in a 1950 catalog.

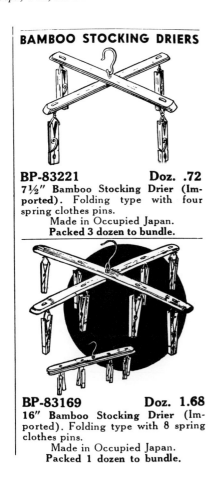

BAMBOO STOCKING DRIERS

BP-83221   **Doz. .72**
7½" Bamboo Stocking Drier (Imported). Folding type with four spring clothes pins.
Made in Occupied Japan.
Packed 3 dozen to bundle.

BP-83169   **Doz. 1.68**
16" Bamboo Stocking Drier (Imported). Folding type with 8 spring clothes pins.
Made in Occupied Japan.
Packed 1 dozen to bundle.

381. Advertisement (1950) for "bamboo stocking driers."

382. Wood salad sets, as shown in a 1950 wholesale catalog.

WOOD SALAD SET

BP-83247   **Doz. Sets .75**
Wood Salad Set (Imported). Spoon and Fork. Length 10". Sanded Beechwood. Each pair banded.
Made in Occupied Japan.
Packed 1 dozen sets to box.

BP-83255   **Doz. .71**
Wood Salad Spoons (Imported). Length 10". Sanded Beechwood.
Made in Occupied Japan.
Packed 1 dozen to box.

supply today. The carved dog-fiddler illustrated here is undoubtedly a member of a larger musical animal group. The piece is only three inches tall, but it is a strong folk carving and it is unfortunate that more were not made. The four dog musicians of carved wood are part of a six-piece band.

Some cloth and yarn items were included in the earliest exhibit of postwar Japanese products. Most were inexpensive sewing notions, such as the velvet-covered strawberry emery or the popular tomato pincushions. Infant booties and sacques were being exported by 1950. These were hand knit, crocheted, or embroidered, and, as one can see from the catalog page reproduced here, were sold at reasonable prices. Silk scarves were also being sold in 1950, but the Japanese found it impossible to bring their silk trade with the United States to its prewar levels. The invention of nylon and the discovery of its remarkable strength and versatility during the war years had made silk obsolete for many domestic purposes.

A very unusual handmade sewing notion is the handsome pincushion shown in Illustrations 389 and 390. It measures six inches across the center, and is a silk hassock of pale pink surrounded by ten silk brocade-clad Japanese babies. All have hand-painted silk faces and black silk-thread pigtails. Each face is a little different, and the

383 **A.** Carved and painted wooden dog fiddler may have been part of a musical group. Height, 4 inches. **B.** Four dog musicians, hand carved and painted, were part of an original group of six. Height, 2½ inches. **A.** *Joseph P. Valenti;* **B.** *Author's Collection*

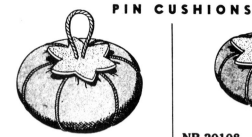

PIN CUSHIONS

NP-20978   **Doz. .50**
Velvet Covered Strawberry Emery. 1½"
long. Made in Occupied Japan.
Packed 2 dozen to box.

NP-20106   **Doz. .75**
Tomato Pin Cushions. 2½" Diameter.
Made in Occupied Japan
Packed 2 dozen to box.

NP-20108   **Doz. .7**
Tomato Pin Cushion and Emery combi
nation. 2¼" Diameter.
Made in Occupied Japan
Packed 2 dozen to box.

384. Catalog advertisement for pincushions and emeries, 1950.

385. Advertisement for hand-knit-ted infants' sacques, from a 1950 wholesale catalog.

HAND KNITTED WOOL SACQUE

HP-5100 R   Doz. 8.50

Hand Knitted All Wool Infants' Sacque. (Imported.) Hand embroidered. Assorted styles. Colors: Pink and Blue.
Made in Occupied Japan.
Packed 1 dozen asst. to box.

HP-38514   Doz. 16.50

Hand Knitted All Wool 3 Piece Infants' Set. (Imported.) Consists of: 1 Sacque, 1 Cap and 1 pair of Bootees. Colors: Pink and Blue. Each set to a box.
Made in Occupied Japan.
Packed 1 dozen assorted.

HAND KNITTED WOOL BOOTEES

HP-38465   Doz. 3.00

Hand Knitted All Wool Bootees. (Imported.) Moccasin type feet. White with Pink and Blue stripes. Self ties.
Made in Occupied Japan.
Packed 3 dozen asst. to box.

HP-38648   Doz. 3.75

Knee Length Hand Knitted All Wool Bootees. (Imported.) Moccasin type feet. White with Pink and Blue trim. Self ties.
Made in Occupied Japan.
Packed 2 dozen asst. to box.

386. Hand-knitted wool booties were available in 1950.

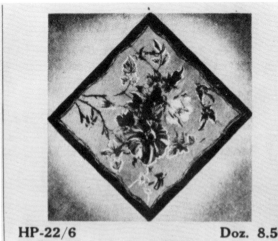

HP-22/6   Doz. 8.50

30″ Pure Silk Scarf. (Imported.) 4½ m/m. Hand rolled edge. Floral and scenic designs. 5 Color prints.
Made in Occupied Japan.
Packed 1 dozen assorted to box.

387. Silk scarves were exported in 1950. These had cloth labels.

SEWING KIT

NP-51901 Doz. 1.25

Sewing Kit. Metal case with pin cushion top. Mirror on inside of lid. Each kit contains six spools colored thread, thimble and needles.
Made in Occupied Japan
Packed 1 dozen to box.

388 A. Advertisement for a sewing kit with a pin-cushion top. **B.** Figural pincushion doll. **B.** *Joseph P. Valenti*

color of each pajama outfit matches the color of the opposite baby's in the circle. The pincushion is a good example of what would today be called soft sculpture. The entire piece is handmade. The mark "Made in Occupied Japan" is stamped on the reverse side.

Pincushions of the type illustrated and described above were exported from both China and Japan in the earlier part of this century, and so it is not known where the idea originated. Similar pincushions are still being made in China, but the faces are stamped and the material used for them is a soft knitted fabric.

Paper garden lanterns of the type in Illustration 392 were made consistently for export with the exception of the war years. Obviously, it is difficult to find many with the Occupied Japan mark. A lantern type that is even more scarce is the round pink collapsible one in Illustrations 393 and 394. As shown, these were marked with a paper sticker. This lantern is eighteen inches in height when opened.

390. Reverse side of the pincushion, showing the stamped mark.

389. Hand-sewn and hand-painted silk pincushion—soft sculpture with damask-clad babies around the edge. *Author's Collection*

391. Wholesale catalog advertisement for needle books made in Occupied Japan.

NP-50180   Doz.
Fancy Needle Books, containing 29 assorted
needles. Each book in glassine envelope
Made in Occupied Japan
Packed 3 dozen books to box.

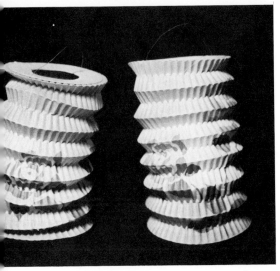

392. Collapsible garden lanterns, approximately 6 inches when opened. *Author's Collection*

393. Paper garden lantern, shocking pink with Japanese calligraphy.

394. Lantern collapses for easy packing and storage. Photo shows the paper label in the bottom.

Full-size silk parasols were undoubtedly brought back to this country by hundreds of the GI's who were stationed in Japan during the Occupation. Only those with the desirable mark were sent to the United States for sale. They are very hard to find today. Accordion paper fans of colorful tissue paper as well as conventional folding fans were exported during the Occupation. One of the fans illustrated was a prize won at a graduation outing held at a Connecticut amusement park. It was dated by its young owner as a remembrance in June of 1949. The reverse side of the fan is stamped "Made in Occupied Japan."

Badly painted papier-mâché wall plaques, trays, coasters, and boxes were a standard inexpensive gift item made by the Japanese. These are often called "lacquer" by those who do not recognize the nature of true Japanese lacquer. A lot of this type of paperware was made, but it had a tendency to peel and crack in overheated American homes; most of it now found is in rather sad condition. Some of the boxes made

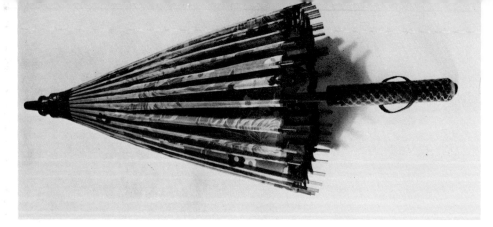

395. Red silk parasol. *Joseph P. Valenti, Jr.*

396. Tiny paper parasols were marked on the paper band that held them closed. *Author's Collection*

from this material were used only as gift boxes for better-made objects. They were too pretty to throw away, and so many have lasted as sewing or notion boxes. Most were decorated with a combination of printing and hand painting.

The Japanese printed a few books in English for the American market, as the now-flourishing Japanese publishing industry struggled to recoup after the war. One title that has been recorded is *Jeeper's Japan*, a book about the Occupation, which was published in Tokyo in 1949. Its author was Francis Baker, and the book has color cartoon illustrations. This is a rare "Occupation" item.

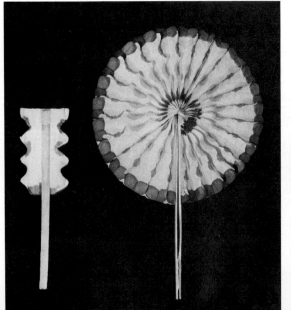

397. Accordion-folded tissue paper fans were used as party favors. *Author's Collection*

398. This paper fan was a prize at an amusement park; its owner dated it "June 21, 1949."

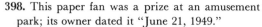

399. Paper fan, printed and hand paint-
ed. Mark is printed
on the reverse side
of an outer rib.

400. Blue silk hand-painted fan marked "Made
in Occupied Japan" on the reverse of an outside rib.

401. Papier-mâché wall plaque with printed and
hand-painted design.

402. Papier-mâché tray in black imitation lacquer with printed and hand-painted decoration.

403. Papier-mâché oval box in gold imitation lacquer with printed and hand-painted decoration. *Author's Collection*

404. Celluloid children's dresser sets as shown in a wholesale catalog for 1950; also, novelty rubber hot water bottles for infants.

IMPORTED, INFANTS' COMB & BRUSH SE

Solid back ivory celluloi
decorated brush with ribb
with fine quality pure white
Beveled saw toothed comb.
ly matched enameled decora
BP-10478   Doz. Se
2 Piece Comb and Brush S
in a gift box, 2⅝" x 4⅝"
Pink and Blue in assorted sh
designs.   **Made in Occupi**
Packed 1 dozen to car

BP-15222   Doz. S
3 Piece Comb, Brush and Po
Set. Each in a gift box, 4¾"
Colors: Pink and Blue in
shapes and designs.
Made in Occupied Jap
Packed 1 dozen to car

BP-15223   Doz. S
3 Piece Comb, Brush and
Set. Each in a gift box, 4¾
Colors: Pink and Blue in
shapes and designs.
Made in Occupied Jap
Packed 1 dozen to car

BP-15224   Doz. S
4 Piece Comb, Brush, Pow
and Tray Set. Each in a gift
x 8½". Colors: Pink and B
sorted shapes and designs.
Made in Occupied Jap
Packed 1 dozen to car

IMPORTED INFANTS' RUBBER HOT WATER BOTT

BP-20530   Do
Infant's Novelty Rubber Hot Water Bottle. Imported. Hand decor
sorted animal shapes. Bear, Cat and Dog. Each in glassine bag. Co
and Blue.
Made in Occupied Japan.
Packed 1 dozen assorted to carton.

There are certainly other paper, wood, and cloth collectibles with the wanted mark. Many articles of this type were used up, stuck in the back of drawers, or thrown out. Today, they are scarce and certainly desirable additions for any comprehensive collection when they can be found in good condition. Those things that were not made to last and that cost so little when new are, perhaps, the rarest of any collectibles marked "Made in Occupied Japan."

15

Dolls and Toys

The Japanese had been able to compete in the American toy market through the period that started at the beginning of this century and continued to the 1930s. Their ingenuity in designing and manufacturing mechanical toys especially was well known, and playthings for children comprised a large part of Japanese exports during the period of the Occupation. There were probably few American children who did not find at least one "Occupied Japan" toy under their Christmas trees in 1950, 1951, and 1952. Even parents who had postwar prejudices about purchasing Japanese products would have been hard put to have a "Made in America" Christmas during those years. Wonderful toys that had been off the market throughout the war years were finally available in quantity at prices that, although higher than prewar, were still low enough to entice even the most patriotic of Americans.

The variety of "Made in Occupied Japan" toys available to American stores in 1950 was large enough to satisfy even buyers of vast quantities of goods for the Christmas season. One wholesale catalog offered at least thirty different dolls in a variety of

405. Doll head of hand-painted porcelain. Body was soft cloth.

sizes, races, and of both sexes. The dolls were made of bisque or celluloid, or had porcelain heads and stuffed soft bodies. Sizes for the bisque dolls ranged from 3½ inches to 5½ inches, and at least one tiny baby doll came with its own wooden cradle and flannel blanket. Many of the bisque dolls were clearly marked on the back either by stamp or impression from the mold. Some of the tiny dolls were fully jointed, but others were made from a single mold.

Celluloid dolls were made in various sizes. The most popular seems to have been the wavy-haired, large-eyed "Betty Boop" variety. These were common amusement park giveaways, and were frequently adorned with a few spangles and feathers. Cuddle dolls with celluloid heads and stuffed bodies were also available. Celluloid rattles and other cute baby toys were made in quantity, but they were eventually taken off the market because they broke easily and small children were likely to put pieces of them in their mouths.

There is an interesting doll that was made in at least three sizes: 2, 4, and 6 inches. It is a replica of a muscular American football player. This doll was sold at football games. It came attached to a team button or to a stick; the smallest had a pin attached to its back. Many of these dolls still have pieces of elastic glued to their necks, and occasionally one can be found still attached to a football team button. The dolls were made in lightweight celluloid in a variety of colors. The larger sizes had jointed arms.

The Occupied Japan toys that are the most difficult to find today are those that were made of rubber. Rubber animals with squeakers were made in some quantity, as were rubber water pistols, rubber daggers, and some inflatable toys. The rubber was not of especially good quality, and the toys rotted easily. The rubber beach balls illustrated here are a rarity, although many collectors would prefer to find some of the animal forms in rubber. An especially desirable item to find today would be the rubber tool kit consisting of wrench, hammer, saw, pliers, hatchet, and screwdriver. These toys once sold wholesale for $1.55 for a dozen kits.

MPORTED CELLULOID TOYS FROM OCCUPIED JAPAN

ALL ITEMS ON THIS PAGE — NET NO DISCOUNT

-20244   Gr. 8.64
le Doll. Height, 3½". Assorted
acked 4 dozen asst'd. to box.

21359/60   Doz. 3.20
ted Celluloid Roly-Poly Dolls.
t from 6½" to 7". Standing
itting Cuddle Dolls with mov-
arms on ball.
cked 1 dozen asst'd. to box.

21390   Gr. 13.80
 Doll. Height, 4¾". Full
d arms and legs. Assorted
cked 2 dozen asst'd. to box.

21391   Gr. 15.00
Doll. Height, 5¼". Full
d arms and legs. Assorted
ed 1 dozen asst'd. to box.

TP-20119   Gr. 9.00
Standing Girl. Height, 4½". Bright
colors. Painted shoes, stockings, and
hat.
Packed 2 dozen to box.

TP-20308   Doz. 1.75
Standing Girl Doll. Height, 6". Painted face, painted hair, and ribbon. Jointed arms.
Packed 1 dozen to box.

TP-20077   Doz. 3.25
Boy and Girl Negro Dolls. Height, 9". Full jointed arms and legs.
Packed 1 dozen asst'd. to box

TP-21291   Doz. 2.25
Standing Boy and Girl Tennis Players Assortment. Height, 7". Holding racket in one hand and ball in the other. Jointed arms. Bright colors.
Packed 1 dozen asst'd. to box.

TP-21411   Doz. 2.00
Cuddle Doll. Height, 6". Full jointed arms and legs. Assorted colors.
Packed 1 dozen asst'd. to box.

TP-20666   Doz. 3.50
Cuddle Doll. Height, 8". Full jointed arms and legs. Assorted colors.
Packed 1 dozen asst'd. to box.

TP-21259   Doz. 1.85
Boy in zippered playsuit. Height, 6". Full jointed arms and legs. Assorted colors.
Packed 1 dozen asst'd. to box.

TP-21258   Doz. 3.75
Boy in zippered playsuit. Height, 8". Full jointed arms and legs. Assorted colors.
Packed 1 dozen asst'd. to box.

TP-21218/9   Gr. 12.00
Celluloid Chick in Egg. 2 colors to assortment. Height, 3½".
Packed 2 dozen asst'd. to box.

TP-3-9-43   Gr. 12.00
Hanging Chick on Egg with ring and string attached. Height, 5".
Packed 1 doz. asst'd. to box.

TP-20736   Gr. 8.75
Sitting Dog. Height, 4". Tongue Sticking out, and wearing bright red bow.
Packed 2 dozen to box.

TP-20341   Gr. 13.20
Floating Dog or Cat in Canoe. One piece. Size, 6". Bright red and yellow.
Packed 1 dozen asst'd. to box.

TP-20334   Gr. 13.20
Dog in Canoe. One piece. Size, 5". Assorted colors.
Packed 1 dozen asst'd. to box.

TP-20354/5   Doz. 1.50
Cat or Bear Assortment. Size, 4½". Movable head. Assorted colors.
Packed 1 dozen asst'd. to box.

TP-20321   Gr. 8.64
Yellow Hen. Height, 3".
Extra heavy celluloid.

TP-20320   Gr. 8.64
Yellow Chick. Height, 3¼". Extra heavy celluloid.
Packed 2 dozen asst'd. to box.

TP-21416   Gr. 8.64
Baseball Animal Assortment. Height, 4¼". 3 animals to assortment.
Packed 2 dozen asst'd. to box

406. Catalog page printed in 1950 shows the great variety of celluloid toys.

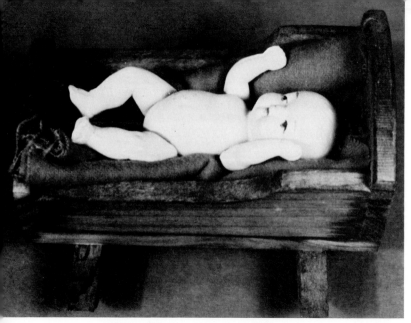

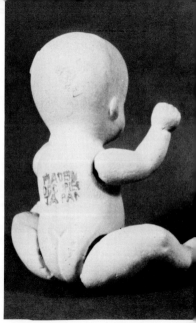

407 & 408. Four-inch bisque doll with jointed arms and legs came with a wooden cradle and flannel blanket. Only the doll is marked.

409 A. Celluloid doll with articulated arms. Height, 5 inches. **B.** Colorful celluloid carnival doll is 10 inches tall. This doll has gold paper tophat, cane, feather costume, and gold glass beads.

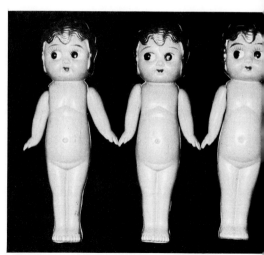

410. Celluloid dolls were carnival giveaways. Height, 8 inches. Mark is embossed on the backs.

411. "Toddling Babe" celluloid windup. *Gary Spadoni*

412. Celluloid football player, 6 inches tall, was attached to a bamboo stick or a team button. *Author's Collection*

413. Miniature football players (2 inches) have pins attached to the back and were sold at football games. Mark is on the seat of the pants.

Undoubtedly, the most desirable of all "Occupied Japan" toys for today's collector are the windup mechanical toys, which were made in a large variety. When key-wound, the animals, automobiles, airplanes, cowboys, and other shapes perform amazingly complicated movements, make a variety of noises, and will entertain for hours. For instance, there is a seal that spins a ball on its nose while sliding along the floor, stopping, and turning around. An amusing gorilla, dressed in a tuxedo, does handstands and other acrobatics. A dancing couple does what might be called the "hesitation waltz," and a "Toddling Babe" walks falteringly around the floor while swinging its arms to keep its balance. A celluloid "Mary" rolls along the floor pulling her white lamb after her.

414. Inflatable beach ball.

IMPORTED TOYS FROM OCCUPIED JAPAN
ALL ITEMS ON THIS PAGE — NET NO DISCOUNT

RUBBER SQUEAK TOYS

TP-21301 Gr. 8.75
Rubber Face Ball with Tongue and Squeaker. Tongue will stick out when ball is squeezed.
Packed 1 dozen to box.

TP-21462/3 Gr. 8.75
Heavy Rubber Dog or Rabbit with Squeaker and Tongue. About 3¾" high.
Packed 1 dozen assorted to box.

RUBBER WATER PISTOL

TP-22138 Gr. 8.00
Rubber Water Pistol. Length, 5". With painted handle and barrel.
Packed 1 dozen to box.

RUBBER DAGGE

TP-21476. Gr.
Rubber Dagger. Length, 6", 3¾" color painted blade and 2¾" black handle.
Packed 1 dozen to box.

TP-21474. Gr.
Rubber Dagger. Length, 7".
TP-21476.
Packed 3 dozen to box.

TP-24326 Gr. 4.50
Rubber Animals with Squeaker. Size, 2½". 4 Assorted styles, Donkey, Dog, Cat and Elephant.
Packed 2 dozen assorted to box.

TP-24630 Gr. 9.60
Rubber Sitting Animals with Squeaker. Size, 3". 3 Assorted styles. Cellophane wrapped.
Packed 1 dozen ass'd. to box.

TP-24635 Gr. 9.60
Rubber Animals with Squeaker. Size, 3". 3 Assorted styles, Chick, Rabbit and Duck.
Packed 1 dozen ass't. to box.

RUBBER MOUSE

TP-20947 Gr. 4.75
Rubber Squeaking Mouse. Color, grey. Overall length 5¼". Tail 2⅝".
Packed 1 dozen to box.

TP-20946 Gr. 8.50
Rubber Squeaking Mouse. Color, grey. Overall length, 7¼". Tail, 3¾".
Packed 2 dozen to box.

TP-20959 Gr.
Rubber Dagger with Sheath. Length, Silver color painted blade and 3" handle, 5" heavy black rubber sheath.
Packed 2 dozen to box.

RUBBER BEACH BALL

TP-21319 Doz.
7" Heavy Rubber Inflated Ball. Assorted colors and designs. Specially constructed valve for inflating and deflating.
Packed 1 dozen to box.

TP-24634 Gr. 9.60
Rubber Animals with Squeaker. Size, 3½". 2 Styles, Rabbit and Duck.
Packed 1 dozen ass'd. to box.

TP-22681 Gr. 12.80
Rubber Animals with Squeaker. Size, 2". 3 Assorted styles, Crocodile, Fish and Tortoise.
Packed 1 dozen assorted to box.

TP-24637 Gr. 13.20
Sitting Rabbit and Duck with Squeaker. Size, 3⅞".
Packed 1 dozen to box.

TP-24636 Gr. 13.20
Rubber Duck with Squeaker. Size, 5". Cellophane wrapped.
Packed 1 dozen to box.

	8 PANEL		
BROWN	Doz.	**COLORE**	
TP-20971	6"	1.85	TP-20182	6
TP-20972	7"	2.10	TP-20183	7
TP-20973	8"	2.60	TP-20184	8
TP-20974	9"	3.25	TP-20185	9
TP-20975	10"	4.00	TP-20186	10
TP-22119	12"	4.75	TP-22150	12

All balls packed 1 dozen of a size to

INFLATABLE RUBBER TOYS

TP-24192 Gr. 7.60
Inflatable Rubber Toys. 4 Assorted styles, Cat, Dog, Elephant and Donkey. Sizes, 6" to 7½".
Packed 4 dozen ass'd. to box.

TP-24215 Gr. 8.64
Inflatable Rubber Toys. 2 Styles, Duck and Hen. Size, 7".
Packed 2 dozen assorted to box.

TP-24191 Gr. 8.64
Inflatable Rubber Toys. 3 Assorted styles, Rooster, Rabbit and Chick. Sizes, 6½" to 8".
Packed 4 dozen assorted to box.

TP-24234 Gr. 14.40
Inflatable Rubber Reindeer. Size, 10".
Packed 2 dozen to box.

TP-24235 Gr. 1
Inflatable Rubber Toys. 3 Assorted, Bear, Elephant, Dog. Sizes 9½" to 12
Packed 2 dozen assorted to box.

415 & 416. Catalog pages of 1950 show toys made of rubber, metal, plush, and bisque.

IMPORTED TOYS FROM OCCUPIED JAPAN
ALL ITEMS ON THIS PAGE — NET NO DISCOUNT

BISQUE DOLLS

TP-90311
Gr. 3.00

Standing Bisque Doll. Height, 3½". Arms wire jointed, gold blonde hair.

Packed 6 dozen to box.

TP-90418
Gr. 5.00

Standing Bisque Girl Doll. Holding animal. Height, 3⅝". Painted shoes, dress and hair ribbon.

Packed 2 dozen to box.

TP-90419
Gr. 5.00

Standing Bisque Boy Doll. With hands in pockets. Height, 3⅝". Painted shoes, coat and cap.

Packed 2 dozen to box.

TP-90310
Gr. 5.50

Standing Bisque Doll. Wearing colored bathing suit with colored bow in hair. Height, 4½". Arms elastic jointed.

Packed 2 dozen to box.

TP-91529
Gr. 5.50

Standing Dressed Bisque Doll. Height, 3½". Assorted color rayon dresses. Arms wire jointed.

Packed 1 dozen to box.

CHIME RATTLES

TP-90309
Gr. 6.80

Standing Bisque Doll. Height, 5". Divided leg. Arms elastic jointed. Golden hair with red ribbon.

Packed 1 dozen to box.

TP-91035
Gr. 13.20

Standing Bisque Doll. Height, 3½". 2 to box. Bright colored rayon dresses.

Packed 1 dozen boxes to carton.

TP-91193 Gr. 14.40

Standing Bisque Doll. Height, 7". Arms jointed. 2 to assortment. One wearing red Painted beret, other with blonde hair.

Packed 2 dozen assorted to box.

TP-90412   **Doz. 1.20**

Big and Little Sister Bisque Doll Set. 2 to box. Large Doll, 4½". Small Doll, 2¾". Assorted bright color rayon dresses.

Packed 1 dozen boxes to carton.

TP-90408
Doz. 1.50

Bisque Doll. Height, 5½". Diaper doll with rubber jointed arms and legs. Flannel diaper with safety pin.

Packed 1½ dozen to box.

P-24299   **Doz. 1.65**

Chime Rattle. Length, 7¼". Baby figures on rattle with attached ring hanging.
Packed 1 dozen to box.

P-21372   **Doz. 2.10**

Chime Rattle. Length, 8¼". Same as P-24299.
Packed 1 dozen to box.

CELLULOID TOY ROCKERS

P-21366   **Doz. 1.90**

Celluloid Elephant or Horse Rocker assortment. Length, 5⅜". Height, Assorted colors.
Packed 1 dozen assorted to box.

METAL SAXOPHONE

P-21461   **Doz. 6.00**

Metal Saxophone. Nickel finish. 8 notes, 8 keys. Wood mouthpiece. Approximate overall length, 13".
Packed ½ dozen to box.

COTTON DOGS

TP-22335   **Doz. 1.80**

Two-Tone Cotton Dogs. Size, 5". Assorted colors. 6 Styles, sitting and standing positions.
Packed 1 dozen assorted to carton.

PLUSH DOGS

TP-22336   **Doz. 2.00**

Two-Tone Rayon Plush Dogs. Size, 5". Assorted colors. 6 Styles, sitting and standing positions.
Packed 1 dozen assorted to carton.

METAL TOY WRIST WATCHES

TP-22108   **Gr. 8.64**

Toy Wrist Watch. All metal with movable hands. Round case, colored dial, metal link band. Each on card.
Packed 6 dozen to box.

TP-22109   **Gr. 9.60**

Toy Wrist Watch. All metal with movable hands. Square case, colored dial, metal link band. Each on card.
Packed 6 dozen to box.

RUBBER TOOL KIT

TP-22714   **Doz. Kits 1.55**

Rubber Tool Kit. 6 Pieces. Consists of wrench, hammer, saw, pliers, hatchet, and screwdriver. Overall length, 7½". Each set mounted on cellophane wrapped card.
Packed 1 dozen kits to box.

FUR MONKEYS

TP-22498 Gr. 6.20

Fur Monkey. Height, 6". Hangs from spring which makes arms and legs movable.
Packed 2 dozen to box.

TP-22235 Gr. 16.50

Fur Monkey. Height, 10". Same as #TP-22498.
Packed 2 dozen to box.

FUR JUMPING DOG

TP-22051   **Doz. 2.10**

Fur Jumping Dog with rubber squeaking ball attached to rubber tube. Jumps when Ball is squeezed. Individually boxed. Approximate overall length, 4".
Packed 1 dozen to box.

ENAMELED BICYCLE HORN

TP-23920   **Doz. 2.40**

Enameled Bicycle Horn. Length, 8". Colors: bright red and bright green. Rubber ball on end and bracket for attachment. Packed 1 dozen assorted to box.

TRAIN SETS

TP-11043   **Gr. 8.40**

4-pc. Toy Train Set. Length, 5". Equally assorted Passenger and Freight train sets. Consists of one engine and 3 cars. Each set individually boxed.
Packed 3 dozen.

IMPORTED MECHANICAL TOYS FROM OCCUPIED JAPAN
ALL ITEMS ON THIS PAGE — NET NO DISCOUNT

WALKING BABY

TP-24253   Doz. 2.40

Mechanical Walking Baby, holding milk bottle. Height 4¼". Individually boxed.

Packed 1 dozen to carton.

CRAWLING BABY

TP-22700   Doz. 3.25

Mechanical Crawling Baby. Polka-dotted dress. Length, 6". Individually boxed.

Packed 1 dozen to carton.

TODDLER

TP-22694   Doz. 5.40

Mechanical Toddler. Polka-dotted dress. Height, 4¾". Individually boxed.

Packed 1 dozen to carton.

WALKING COOK BOY

TP-24197   Doz. 2.40

Mechanical Walking Cook Boy. Height, 4¼". Individually boxed.

Packed 1 dozen to carton.

JUGGLING BEAR   **MERRY-GO-ROUND**

   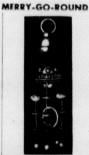

TP-24698 Doz. 3.60   TP-24683 Doz. 3.75

Mechanical Juggling Bear. Height, 6¼". Individually boxed.

Packed 1 dozen to carton.

Mechanical Merry-Go-Round, with bird in cage. Length, 12½". Individually boxed.

Packed 1 dozen to carton.

WALKING DOG   **PECKING CHICK**

TP-24680 Doz. 3.00   TP-24233 Doz. 3.50

Mechanical Walking "Scotty" Dog holding Man's Hat. Length, 4". Individually boxed.

Packed 1 dozen to carton.

Mechanical Pecking Chick. Attractively colored. Height, 3¼". Individually boxed.

Packed 1 dozen to carton.

JUGGLER

TP-24249   Doz. 2.65

Mechanical Juggler. Attractively colored. Height, 4½", with 3" stick and plate. Individually boxed.

Packed 1 dozen to carton.

CLOWN

TP-24250   Doz. 4.80

Mechanical Clown with Twirling Stick. Attractively colored. Height 5½". Individually boxed.

Packed 1 dozen to carton.

ROBOT

TP-22068   Doz. 4.2

Mechanical Robot. Construction Heavy metal, with movable arm. Painted dials on body. Height, approx. 5". Individually boxed.

Packed 1 dozen to carton.

TIPSY SAILOR

TP-24396   Doz. 4.4

Mechanical Tipsy Sailor. Height, 6". Attractively colored. Individually boxed.

Packed 1 dozen to carton.

KANGAROO

TP-24681   Doz. 3.0

Mechanical Jumping Kangaroo. Height, 3½" with 2½" rubber tail. Individually boxed.

Packed 1 dozen to carton.

SIGNAL CAR

TP-21766   Doz. 5.20

Mechanical Signal Car. All metal. When car is in motion, it turns automatically and driver extends arm and signals. Length, 5". Individually boxed.

Packed 1 dozen to carton.

CAT AND BUTTERFLY

TP-24678   Doz. 3.00

Mechanical Cat chasing Butterfly. Length, 4¼". Individually boxed.

Packed 1 dozen to carton.

ROLL-OVER CAT

TP-22701   Doz. 6.60

Mechanical Roll-Over Cat. Plush covered. Assorted colors. Length, 6". Individually boxed.

Packed 1 dozen to carton.

COWBOY

TP-21502   Doz. 5.2

Mechanical Cowboy. All metal brown horse with leather tail and celluloid adjustable cowboy; gun in one hand, holding reins with other. Length, Height, 5¾". Individually boxed.

Packed 1 dozen to carton.

417. Catalog page, 1950, shows some of the toys made in Occupied Japan that were mechanical.

418. "Trick Seal" struts around and twirls a ball on its nose when wound. *Gary Spadoni*

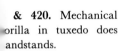

& 420. Mechanical orilla in tuxedo does andstands.

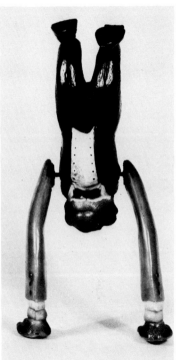

421. "Dancing Couple" celluloid windup with the original box. *Gary Spadoni*

422 A. Celluloid "Mary and Her Lamb" windup toy moves on wheels. B. Windup celluloid dog wags head and tail. A. *Peter's Antiques;* B. *Joseph P. Valenti*

When wound, a metal skier pushes himself rather frantically along with his ski poles, and a red-nosed drunk figure tumbles and twirls across the floor. A little metal chick in a derby hat flaps its wings and pecks. A plush-covered cat rolls over and tumbles with the ball it holds between its front paws, and a mechanical kangaroo hops across the floor in giant leaps.

423. Crosscountry skier pushes himself along on wheeled skis. *Gary Spadoni*

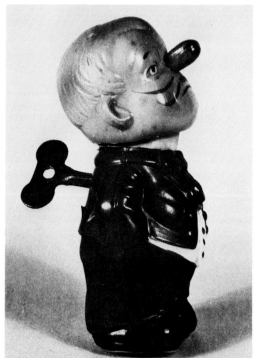

424. Mechanical drunk totters around when wound. *Gary Spadoni*

425. Pecking chick mechanical toy. *Gary Spadoni*

The Japanese seemed to understand the American's love affair with automobiles, and made many toy cars with a variety of mechanical movements. A small figure in a "Signal car" drives a short distance, the driver signals a left turn, and the car turns after the signal is given. Another figure in a car called "Justa Shmoe" leans forward when the car goes forward; when the automobile reverses itself, the figure leans back. An aviator in a plane turns around in his cockpit while the plane whirls around from a suspended string. One mechanical toy that was advanced for its time is a heavy metal walking robot.

Among the prime collector's items in windup toys is a "GI Joe," a round-faced, pink-cheeked soldier that crawls along on its stomach, stops, and shoots its rifle at some imaginary enemy (which, only a few years previous to its manufacture, might have been its maker), and then repeats the cycle until he requires further winding. A mechanical figure with a similar movement is the American cowboy windup dressed in kerchief, chaps, and holster, which walks along, stops, and shoots its guns, and then repeats the motion.

426. "Signal car" mechanical toy. *Gary Spadoni*

427. "Justa Shmoe" mechanical toy. *Gary Spadoni*

428. "GI Joe" moves along on stomach, stops, and shoots rifle. *Gary Spadoni*

A miniature windup tricycle really works and has a bell that rings, and a motorcycle with rider rears up on its back wheel intermittently while speeding in circles around the floor. There were many other mechanical wheel products. Some of these were replicas of real American automobiles of the early 1950s, and others are army vehicles, especially the Jeep, with which postwar Japanese citizens were all too familiar.

Toy watches, inexpensive metal musical instruments, bicycle horns, games, and puzzles were also the delight of many children during the period of the Occupation. Doll dishes, dollhouse furniture, and many other miniature items were available from Japan for the first time in many years. A rare item is the Japanese lead soldier on horseback, which was undoubtedly part of a set when it was new.

430. Red mechanical tricycle drives around and rings its own bell. *Gary Spadoni*

429. Shooting cowboy mechanical toy. *Gary Spadoni*

431. "Auto cycle" rears up on its back wheel. Shown with the original box. *Gary Spadoni*

432. Group of toy automobiles, all marked "Made in Occupied Japan." *Gary Spadoni*

433. Samurai warrior is brightly painted lead. Mark is embossed on the belly of the horse and on the bottom of the stand. Sword is missing from the hand. *Author's Collection*

434. Plane hangs from a string, and when wound, travels around in wide circles while the pilot looks behind him. *Gary Spadoni*

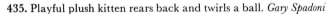

435. Playful plush kitten rears back and twirls a ball. *Gary Spadoni*

Although a quarter century of age is not considered "old" in many categories of collecting, toy collectors are aware that only a small percentage of toys made during any era manage to last very long in good condition. Many of the mechanical toys that sold for less than one dollar in 1950 are now bringing surprisingly high prices. This is especially true if the toys are in pristine condition and are in their original boxes. Collectors will pay premium prices if the windup key is included, since this was often lost among the Christmas wrappings, and such keys are in short supply today. All toys marked "Made in Occupied Japan" have become valuable collector's items and are presently worthwhile investments for the future.

436. Plush mechanical dog, a little the worse for wear, barks and begs. A cloth label is sewn in the stomach seam. *Peter Tavera*

437. "Puzzle Ring" game, complete with box and instructions, is a rarity.

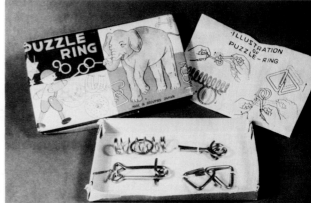

438. Four-piece toy train set is a miniature; an advertisement for other sets can be seen at bottom of Ill. 415. *Author's Collection*

439. Adult toy, a squirting lapel flower. The flower is celluloid, and was made in pale or deep pink and white. Bulb is rubber. Marked "Made in Occupied Japan" on the bulb and "Japan" on the flower.

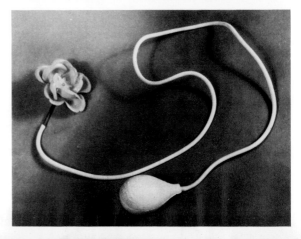

440. Toy tea set in popular Willow pattern.

441. Toy tea set with decalcomania decoration.

16

Glass

The collector searching for "Occupied Japan" glass objects today will find it is next to impossible to find more than one or two pieces. There are several good reasons why so few glass articles were made. The United States has always been a glass-producing country, and there would have been little sense in the Japanese attempting to create a market for glassware in a country where manufacturers were not only competitive but certainly also disgruntled to have competition for their own products.

Most of the pressed glass items found with the "Made in Occupied Japan" mark are perfume or cologne atomizers, and these were probably commissioned as containers for a company that sold them filled and boxed. They are made in colored or clear glass in designs strongly reminiscent of the thirties. The molds were probably left over from before the war, and the necessary mark on the bases of these pieces was simply cut into the existing molds. The rubber part of the atomizer screw tops was of such poor quality that it has generally broken off and been discarded, but the bottles themselves are heavy glass of commercial quality.

442. Pressed glass cologne bottle is embossed on the base "Made in Occupied Japan."

443. Cologne or perfume bottles in clear and pink pressed glass. Mark is embossed on the bottom of both.

In addition to glass bottles, a few glass jars were made to be used for mayonnaise or mustard. Probably these were once parts of sets that included salt and pepper shakers. The shaker sets can be found in limited quantity in glass. Those most often found are cobalt blue glass containers with metal tops, set inside a casing of white metal.

There should be no misunderstanding that the scarcity of glass objects made during the Occupation for export is evidence that the Japanese were not capable of manufacturing fine glass. The lenses for binoculars and cameras attest to the fact that glassmaking was well within the capabilities of the Japanese, and Japan still leads the world in the manufacture of fine optical products.

O.J. glass collectibles include some toy dishes and especially cups and saucers made in white opaque glass, which may be mistaken for porcelain. Mostly, these items were made to sell for pennies; the cups and saucers shown in Illustration 447 with the

444 A. Pressed glass mustard jar with wooden cover is impressed on the base, "Made in Occupied Japan." **B.** Pressed glass shakers with metal tops are also marked on the bases.

446 A. Metal with blue glass inserts, the shakers are on metal tray with red plastic handles and knobs. B. White metal encases a cobalt blue glass insert on this table lighter.

445. Covered metal dish has a cobalt blue insert.

original box and packing are not very good quality, but are somewhat scarce only because so little glass was exported. The decorations, although colorful, are decals.

The glass and metal object shown in Illustrations 448 and 449 is evidence of how the Japanese struggled to find products that might be suitable for export during the early days of the Occupation. The set of glass and metal rosary beads was probably made well before the war for export. Each blue glass bead is encased in a thin white or gold-colored metal filigree. The center medallion is of white metal of fairly good quality, well embossed and heavy. The crucifix, however, is of the thinnest metal, and is easily bent. Its only decoration is the familiar mark, "Made in Occupied Japan." Undoubtedly, the Japanese manufacturer or jobber who found these beads and thought them suitable for export was hard put to find a place where the beads could be marked. He probably removed the original crucifix and added the new one. If a collector is interested in unusual objects that represent the period in history under discussion, certainly this string of rosary beads is a great oddity. Perhaps the American importer was supposed to replace the cross once the beads were safely through customs. However, at least one group of them, with the metal cross in both gold and silver finish, remained as they were. Obviously, these beads display the most unusual use of the "Made in Occupied Japan" mark that one might find. Most undoubtedly remained unsold on the unfortunate importer's shelf until current collectors began to search for anything with the "Occupied" mark.

Beads for fashion rather than religious purposes were made too. These are almost impossible to identify today, since the marks were usually on the paper label or on the

447. White opaque glass miniature cups and saucers with decalcomania decoration, shown with their original box.

448 & 449. Medium blue cut glass rosary beads encased in pierced metal. One of the most unusual items found so far, the beads have a thin metal cross marked "Made in Occupied Japan."

box in which they were packed. The same is true of strings of buttons. Other glass fashion trimmings were probably made as well. Collectors may never be able to identify many of the smaller objects on which the mark was placed elsewhere in the packings or on a separate label.

Some of the earliest consumer items sent to the United States were Christmas tree ornaments. These were fragile items, many of them made of thin blown glass, and few of them can be found today. The two ornaments illustrated here have their paper labels intact. Both are made from strips of beaded glass with a silver or gold coating. Although used by the same family each year as tree ornaments, the paper labels were never removed. Christmas tree lights and bulbs were made in some quantity during the Occupation. Strings of glass rods and beads were also sold as tree ornaments. These are segments of colored and clear glass rods interspersed with metallic-coated round and oval beads. They too were marked with a paper label.

Tiny glass animals in a variety of colors were made and sold as assortments at the low wholesale price of seventy cents a dozen. Most of these were marked only on the box, and are hard to identify now. The small blue glass cat illustrated is a rarity. Single animals and "families" of three to five pieces were made. All the glass animals were miniatures measuring at the most 2½ inches in length.

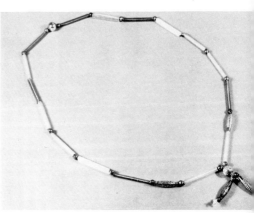

450. Christmas tree decoration made of glass balls and beaded glass rods. Both have the original paper labels attached. *Priscilla and Edward Holt*

451. Christmas tree decoration made of segments of glass rods and metallic coated glass beads.

48   Manufacturers   NEW YORK MERCHANDISE COMPANY, Inc.   Exporters—Importers

MINIATURES AND NOVELTIES — MADE IN OCCUPIED JAPAN
ALL ITEMS ON THIS PAGE — NET NO DISCOUNT

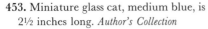

BP-22308A   Doz. .73   **BP-11587**   Doz. .70
Imitation Miniature Ivory Carvings on black plastic and walnut wood base.   Glass Animal Assortment. Sizes up to 2½" long. Beautiful variety.
Size of base, approximately 2¼". Regular 25 cent values.   Packed 1 dozen assorted colors and assorted subjects to box.
        Packed 1 dozen of each subject. Minimum shipment 6 dozen.

BP-1182A   Doz. Sets 1.50
Glass Animal Family Sets. Consists of Elephants, Penguins, Ducks, Chickens, Dogs, etc.
3 to 5 pieces to set. Sizes up to 2".
        Packed 3 dozen assorted sets.

452. Catalog advertisement for miniature glass animals and "animal families." The advertisement also shows miniature "imitation ivory" (plastic) carvings.

453. Miniature glass cat, medium blue, is 2½ inches long. *Author's Collection*

454. Wholesale catalog advertisement for crystal glass stemware.

CRYSTAL GLASS STEMWARE

BP-11168   **Case lots only   Doz**
Crystal Glass Stemware. Cut in beautiful all over floral design. 6 Glasses of c
to a strong corrugated carton. Packed 6 dozen each of the following to case:
Sherbet, Cocktail, Wine and Liquor Glasses.
        30 dozen to case.

Perhaps the greatest surprise for O.J. or glass collectors will be the crystal glass stemware illustration taken from a 1950 wholesaler's catalog. This stemware was included on a catalog page headed "China and Glassware Made in Occupied Japan," which says that stemware cut in floral designs was made in five sizes. However, it was probably not sold in very large amounts. It was marked either with a paper sticker or with an etched mark in the base. Even one of these pieces of stemware would be a major find for any collector today.

455. Figural bottle in the shape of a knight on horseback. The label reads, "Imperial Knight Apricot Liqueur/ Artificially Colored/ 60 Proof 1 oz/ Prepared and Bottled by Federal Liqueurs Ltd. Cambridge Mass." On the base of the bottle is embossed "Bottle Made in Occupied Japan." Ground stopper, clear glass.

456. Owl lamp, 5 inches in height, is made of frosted glass and is battery operated. The lamp has a chrome base. *Anna Decker*

457. Miniature glass animals. Largest is 1½ inches long. They have a pearlized finish. *Margie Grustas*

17

"Made in Occupied Japan" Collectibles as an Investment

If you had the foresight to start collecting all objects marked "Made in Occupied Japan" as recently as 1970, you are aware that no popular collectible has risen in value as quickly as this diversified category. Yet there is a great amount of confusion among both dealers and collectors as to how much one should pay for many of the objects and whether they will increase in value with time. The few price guides presently available have such disparity in prices for similar objects that they have confused many new collectors and discouraged others.

In one price guide published in 1972, for instance, Satsuma-type miniature vases (2½ inches) are listed as being worth $12.50 each, but in another price guide published in 1976, the same vase is listed as selling for $3. A single bisque figurine, 7 inches in height, may show up in one price guide for $40, whereas a more recent guide will list the identical good-quality "Made in Occupied Japan" figurine for less than half that amount. A collector who pursues this hobby with the idea that the objects will increase in value over the years can be hard put to know which price guide to believe.

In any collecting category, especially one as recent as "Occupied Japan" objects, the collector who is just starting out should be suspicious of any price guide compiled by dealer-collectors. They are prone to price the things in their own collections at high and sometimes unrealistic levels in order to glorify the value of things they already own. Frequently, the prices in this type of guide are only wishful thinking on the part of the owner.

There is, of course, only one basic factor that sets the prices of all commodities, and that is supply and demand. Only a few years ago, most items marked "Made in Occupied Japan" were quite plentiful, although there certainly were more porcelain figurines in smaller sizes than pieces in any other category. As more and more collectors and dealers began to consider the investment potential in Japanese products made for export to the United States during the Occupation, the scarcer and better-made bisque and porcelain figurines, vases, and dishes began to disappear from dealers' shelves and the prices began to rise. Obviously, those items that are well made and in short supply will continue to rise in value. Not a great number of the finer figurines were made, and a lot have been broken over the years. As the better pieces became more difficult to find, the smaller "Occupied" bisque and porcelain figurines that were available in much greater quantity also began to be collected and they are still being sought. Although collectors were buying a mark, they looked for items that had special appeal.

Since not as many glass, wood, or metal objects were made—and many collectors were unaware of the scarcity of some of these items—prices for them remained relatively low. The aesthetic appeal of some of these items is not as strong for collectors, and often dealers do not even know that the "Made in Occupied Japan" mark on a white metal ashtray can boost its value to double or triple what it might have brought without the mark.

458. Pair of Japanese dolls with hand-painted composition faces, real hair, and brocade costumes. The male doll has a paper hat with hand embroidery; the back of the kimono is hand painted. Both dolls are marked on the bottom in purple ink: "Made in Occupied Japan." *Author's Collection*

459. Porcelain clock case with raised flowers. The clock was to be installed by Gilbert Clock Company of Winsted, Connecticut, but it was never put in. *Anna Decker*

For the unusual items in paper or cloth, many collectors will gladly pay any price. Most of these were disposable, and so they are in short supply. Therefore, the price for a paper lantern with its original sticker may be higher than that for a reasonably good piece of bisque. Presently, wholesalers who sell to antique dealers and flea market dealers are urging novelty store owners who have been in business since the war in the same location to search their stockrooms for long-forgotten boxes of items with the desirable mark. Once the Occupation was over and Japan was on her own, anything unsold that was marked "Made in Occupied Japan" was pushed aside and new stock took its place. There is still a lot to be found. A quarter century is, after all, not a long period of time in collectibles.

If collectors find fictitiously high prices on some categories of O.J. collectibles, they will also find that values for a few categories in some price guides are unrealistically low. This situation results from the fact that the "Occupied Japan" collector must compete with other specialist-collectors in some areas. Bisque dolls, for instance, are in demand by many people who are not especially interested in the "Occupied Japan" mark, but who realize that a doll that can be dated within a period of four or five years has good investment potential. They also want the tiny bisque dolls because they are no longer being made and they have become desirable as dollhouse characters. The same is true of celluloid dolls. Many of both these types of dolls were made, but relatively few survived.

Mechanical toys are another category for which there is much competition. Toys and games do not have to be very old to be collectible. The mechanical windups made during the Occupation are especially appealing, both to "Occupied Japan" collectors and collectors of old toys.

There are, of course, numerous people who collect odd cups and saucers, and the huge variety of sizes and types will appeal to thousands of collectors, who will buy them with or without the O.J. mark if they are pretty and inexpensive. Certainly, thousands of American women amass huge collections of novelty salt and pepper shaker sets, and it would surprise many of them to know that those marked "Made in Occupied Japan" are worth much more than the 25¢ they paid for them when they were new.

460. Bisque boudoir lamp with glass chimney and bisque shade. *Anna Decker*

461. Card of pearlized buttons, an extremely rare find. Buttons were exported in larger quantities on strings and marked with paper labels. *Margie Grustas*

462. Birdcage clock, gold and chrome metal, has 30-hour movement. Numbered ball turns in the cage, and bird turns back and forth with each tick. Cage is removable from marble and metal stand. Mark is impressed in chrome disk on base and on bottom of cage. Height, 8½ inches. *Author's Collection*

There is also competition from other collecting areas that can drive up the prices of certain "Made in Occupied Japan" objects. A cigarette lighter made in the shape of a camera on a tripod is a "photographica" collectible. The same is true of the obsolete and ingenious miniature real cameras made in Japan after the war. Box collectors search for good-quality Oriental lacquer, and will not care at all if a box they like might have been made during the Occupation.

In most collecting fields a good practice to follow, when deciding what ceiling to place on your investments, is to consider whether the item was of good quality when it was new and had some artistic merit then. If it qualified on those criteria, it would be worth more now as a collectible. Obviously, this does not always hold true for "Made in Occupied Japan" collectibles. Very little was made that was expensive or artistically designed when new. Certainly, the better bisque and porcelain figurines, the fine chinaware, and the more carefully produced lacquerware will always be the best pieces in any O.J. collection. The few pieces of pottery made in contemporary style and marked Noritake china will rise in value as more and more collectors strive to upgrade their collections.

Yet there are many other items that will continue to escalate in value although originally they were in the five-and-dime category of Japanese products made after the war. All objects with an American theme, such as the Uncle Sam figurines, cowboys, or Indians, figurines of blacks, and especially the toby mug of General MacArthur, fall into this valuable category.

There are thousands of collectors of miniatures, and since this is a type of manufacture in which the Japanese have excelled for many years, there is great demand for the tiny tea sets and other such objects made in some quantity during the Occupation. All miniatures are easily lost or broken, and porcelain clocks, lamps, and dollhouse furniture are scarce. Those marked "Made in Occupied Japan" are especially difficult to find—this is another case where an item that sold for pennies now brings dollars.

It will be some time before all objects made during the Occupation will be known. The entire area of O.J. collecting is exciting in that there are constant surprises for the determined collector. At this early stage of what promises to be one of the most exciting new collecting hobbies, you can still find objects marked "Made in Occupied Japan" to suit any budget. They are still available in every area of the United States. Buy only those pieces that are in perfect condition. If the original box is available, so much the better.

A mark that was once punitive and a stigma on boatloads of merchandise is now recognized by many to represent an interesting, if sad, period in Japanese-American political and business history. The collecting of objects marked "Made in Occupied Japan" promises to be a challenging and fascinating hobby for many years to come. It is also, without doubt, an investment opportunity that will result in valuable profits in the future.

Index

Italic figures refer to illustrations.